YIELDS ON CORPORATE DEBT
DIRECTLY PLACED

NATIONAL BUREAU OF ECONOMIC RESEARCH

Number 84, General Series

YIELDS ON CORPORATE DEBT DIRECTLY PLACED

By AVERY B. COHAN

UNIVERSITY OF NORTH CAROLINA

NATIONAL BUREAU OF ECONOMIC RESEARCH
NEW YORK 1967

Distributed by COLUMBIA UNIVERSITY PRESS
NEW YORK & LONDON

196327

RELATION OF THE DIRECTORS TO THE WORK AND PUBLICATIONS OF THE NATIONAL BUREAU OF ECONOMIC RESEARCH

1. The object of the National Bureau of Economic Research is to ascertain and to present to the public important economic facts and their interpretation in a scientific and impartial manner. The Board of Directors is charged with the responsibility of ensuring that the work of the National Bureau is carried on in strict conformity with this object.

2. To this end the Board of Directors shall appoint one or more Directors of Research.

3. The Director or Directors of Research shall submit to the members of the Board, or to its Executive Committee, for their formal adoption, all specific proposals concerning researches to be instituted.

4. No report shall be published until the Director or Directors of Research shall have submitted to the Board a summary drawing attention to the character of the data and their utilization in the report, the nature and treatment of the problems involved, the main conclusions, and such other information as in their opinion would serve to determine the suitability of the report for publication in accordance with the principles of the National Bureau.

5. A copy of any manuscript proposed for publication shall also be submitted to each member of the Board. For each manuscript to be so submitted a special committee shall be appointed by the President, or at his designation by the Executive Director, consisting of three Directors selected as nearly as may be one from each general division of the Board. The names of the special manuscript committee shall be stated to each Director when the summary and report described in paragraph (4) are sent to him. It shall be the duty of each member of the committee to read the manuscript. If each member of the special committee signifies his approval within thirty days, the manuscript may be published. If each member of the special committee has not signified his approval within thirty days of the transmittal of the report and manuscript, the Director of Research shall then notify each member of the Board, requesting approval or disapproval of publication, and thirty additional days shall be granted for this purpose. The manuscript shall then not be published unless at least a majority of the entire Board and a two-thirds majority of those members of the Board who shall have voted on the proposal within the time fixed for the receipt of votes on the publication proposed shall have approved.

6. No manuscript may be published, though approved by each member of the special committee, until forty-five days have elapsed from the transmittal of the summary and report. The interval is allowed for the receipt of any memorandum of dissent or reservation, together with a brief statement of his reasons, that any member may wish to express; and such memorandum of dissent or reservation shall be published with the manuscript if he so desires. Publication does not, however, imply that each member of the Board has read the manuscript, or that either members of the Board in general, or of the special committee, have passed upon its validity in every detail.

7. A copy of this resolution shall, unless otherwise determined by the Board, be printed in each copy of every National Bureau book.

(Resolution adopted October 25, 1926, as revised February 6, 1933, and February 24, 1941)

This report is one of a series emerging from an investigation of interest rates made possible by a grant to the National Bureau from the Life Insurance Association of America. The Association is not, however, responsible for any of the statements made or views expressed.

ADVISORY COMMITTEE ON THE
INTEREST RATES STUDY

In the planning and review of its studies of interest rates, the National Bureau has benefited from the advice and guidance of this committee. The committee's concurrence with the views expressed in this report, however, is not to be assumed. The members of the committee are:

CONTENTS

TABLES

CHARTS

PREFACE

This study is, in a sense, a lineal descendant of David Durand's study of basic yields on corporate bonds. Durand's purpose was to construct homogeneous series on basic yields—series, that is, which would be free of "extraneous" influences and which, therefore, would represent to the greatest possible extent the pure movement through time of yields on the "best" bonds. My purpose in this study has been to construct series which would represent the pure movement through time of yields on various homogeneous classes of direct placements.

By and large, such techniques as I have used have been directed to identifying those characteristics of a new direct placement which are relevant to variations in yield, *time held constant*, and which, therefore, should be held constant *through time* if the resulting series are to be reasonably homogeneous.

The problem of identifying such "relevant" characteristics, especially when dynamic influences are present, is not as simple as it may seem. And the chances are that, if I were to do this study again, I would not do it in quite the same way. I do hope, however, that other workers on this and similar problems will find some stimulation in the approach.

In bringing this study to completion I have incurred a multitude of obligations, only a few of which can be acknowledged here.

The greatest of these are to the late Joseph W. Conard, who persuaded the National Bureau to undertake the study, to James J. O'Leary, who persuaded the Life Insurance Association of America to provide the necessary financial support and who, himself, provided help and counsel at every step of the way, and to those life insurance companies which agreed to supply the data on which the study is based. Without the support of Professor

Conard, Dr. O'Leary and the LIAA, or the industry itself, the study could not have been undertaken.

I am indebted, next, to the National Bureau's staff reading committee—Jack M. Guttentag, F. Thomas Juster, and Geoffrey H. Moore—all of whom devoted much time and energy to the various preliminary versions of the manuscript. The final version is almost as much their product as mine, and I cannot honestly, therefore, take full credit for whatever virtues it may possess.

The members of the National Bureau's Advisory Committee on the Interest Rates Study are listed on a previous page. Every member of the committee has contributed something to the study, but of those who have not been acknowledged above, W. Braddock Hickman, Milton Friedman, Sidney Homer, and George T. Conklin were especially helpful.

I am grateful also to the reading committee of the National Bureau's Board of Directors: Walter E. Hoadley, Willis J. Winn, and Donald B. Woodward. J. Wilson Newman of the Board also provided a helpful comment.

Help in collecting and processing data was provided by an able succession of research assistants: William Hardin, Jr. (now Associate Professor of Finance at Virginia Polytechnic Institute), Luther H. Hodges, Jr. (now a senior vice-president of the North Carolina National Bank), Lois Terrill, Judith Hamburger, John Beverly, Arch T. Allen, Ronnie Anderson, Richard McEnally, Stephen Hu, and William C. Hale.

As indicated above, the major portion of the financial support for the study was provided by the LIAA. Several other organizations, however, contributed in various ways: the Graduate School of Business Administration of the University of North Carolina, the Research Computation Center of the University of North Carolina, and the Management Development Institute (IMEDE), Lausanne, Switzerland.

Joan Tron has edited the manuscript with great patience, skill, and understanding; H. Irving Forman drew the charts.

FOREWORD

In this study, Professor Cohan sets himself the task of constructing time series on the yields of directly placed corporate bonds that will be relatively homogeneous over time with respect to the many borrower and transaction characteristics that affect yields on different obligations. Although, as Cohan states in his preface, this is a direct descendant of Durand's work on basic yields, the statistical technique employed is a product of our computer age and would hardly have been feasible when Durand began his study. In contrast to the technique of computing basic yields, which results in a single homogeneous series covering the "best" securities and which in effect discards information on other securities, Cohan's multiple regression technique results in a number of relatively homogeneous series, towards which every observation makes its direct contribution. Each of these series is defined in terms of an unchanged bundle of yield-determining characteristics, and these bundles can be scaled in a variety of ways to meet different purposes. Cohan contents himself with three series based on sets of characteristics derived from "cross-classified" series, but this does not begin to exhaust the potential inherent in the technique.

This book, then, is really two things. It is first a technical manual on how to construct homogeneous yield series. In this respect it is frankly experimental. Cohan concedes, as must inevitably be the case in a study of this sort, that if he were to do it again he would probably do some things differently. Students dealing with other kinds of yield data will surely profit by studying Cohan's technique, but they may find that their own data call for somewhat different treatment. Cohan's procedure is most appropriate when the underlying yield data have a substantial degree of cross-section variability, and when the mix of yield-determining characteristics is unstable; the technique is feasible only when there is sufficient collateral data to explain a good part of the cross-section variability. Cohan's results, nevertheless, will be useful to other students faced with the question of whether a similar kind of adjustment would materially affect their own series.

But Cohan's work is more than just a technical manual; it also fills a statistical gap of major proportions. When the National Bureau began its study of interest rates, it was decided that a portion of the work should be devoted to removing statistical data deficiencies for two major instruments: directly placed corporate bonds and mortgages on both residential and nonresidential properties. With these gaps eliminated, various possibilities open for fruitful analytical work. In one direction such work can lead to better evaluation of the efficiency of these markets, from the standpoint of resource allocation and the transmission of monetary policy effects. In another direction, possibilities arise for studying the influence of rates and other loan terms on economic activity with respect to sectors defined fairly narrowly, with the financial data corresponding more closely than has heretofore been possible to the cost and availability conditions faced by the specific sector. Cohan's work, therefore, can be expected to yield analytical dividends well beyond those encompassed in the present volume. These analytical uses of the data, as well as their practical value to the financial community, would be enhanced if Cohan's series were brought up-to-date and maintained currently. It is to be hoped that some interested organization, perhaps the SEC itself, will undertake this task.

JACK M. GUTTENTAG

EDITOR'S NOTE: The actual averages have now been brought through 1963 with the generous assistance of Robert H. Menke of the SEC and his staff—but unhappily too late for inclusion in this volume.

1

INTRODUCTION AND SUMMARY

The growth of direct placements has been one of the most striking developments, since the mid-thirties, in the market for long-term capital. Direct placements are long-term loans made directly to business by life insurance companies and pension and mutual funds.[1]

In the thirty-four years from 1900 to 1934, about 3 per cent of all corporate debt cash offerings, or approximately $1 billion, were directly placed. However, in the ensuing thirty-one years, from 1935 to 1965, 46 per cent, or $85 billion, were directly placed.[2]

This growth is shown in detail, both in absolute terms and relative to the growth of public offerings, in Tables 1 through 5. These tables indicate that industrials, utilities, and rails have contributed by no means equally to the total growth of direct placements.

Industrial direct placements have grown by far the most, both in absolute terms and relative to public offerings (Table 2). In recent years they have accounted for more than 70 per cent of all corporate direct placements (Table 5) [3] and have constituted as much as 91 per cent of all industrial cash debt offerings (Table 2). Since 1951, they have fluctuated between 46 per cent (1958) and 85 per cent (1951) of all such offerings.

[1] For detailed definition, see below, p. 8.

[2] The figures for the earlier period were derived from data given in W. B. Hickman, *The Volume of Corporate Bond Financing Since 1900,* Princeton University Press, for National Bureau of Economic Research, 1953. Table A-10. Data for the later period are from *32nd Annual Report of the Securities and Exchange Commission, 1966.* Table 5.

[3] Including the issues of finance companies.

TABLE 1

Total Corporate Debt Cash Issues, Publicly Offered and Directly Placed, 1935–65
(dollar figures in millions)

Year	Publicly[a] Offered	Directly Placed	Total	Per Cent Directly Placed
1935	1,840	385	2,225	17
1936	3,660	369	4,029	9
1937	1,291	327	1,618	20
1938	1,353	691	2,044	34
1939	1,276	703	1,979	36
1940	1,628	758	2,386	32
1941	1,578	811	2,389	34
1942	506	411	917	45
1943	621	369	990	37
1944	1,892	778	2,670	29
1945	3,851	1,004	4,855	21
1946	3,019	1,863	4,882	38
1947	2,889	2,147	5,036	43
1948	2,965	3,008	5,973	50
1949	2,437	2,453	4,890	50
1950	2,360	2,560	4,920	52
1951	2,364	3,326	5,690	58
1952	3,645	3,957	7,601	52
1953	3,856	3,228	7,083	46
1954	4,003	3,484	7,488	46
1955	4,119	3,301	7,420	44
1956	4,225	3,777	8,002	47
1957	6,118	3,839	9,957	39
1958	6,332	3,320	9,653	34
1959	3,557	3,632	7,190	50
1960	4,806	3,275	8,081	40
1961	4,706	4,720	9,425	50
1962	4,487	4,516	9,016	50
1963	4,714	6,158	10,872	57
1964	3,623	7,243	10,865	67
1965	5,570	8,150	13,720	59

Note: In Tables 1 through 4 and Table 6, detail will not always add to total due to rounding.

Source: Securities and Exchange Commission.

[a]Includes railway equipment trust certificates.

TABLE 2

Industrial, Financial, and Service: Total Debt Cash Issues,
Publicly Offered and Directly Placed, 1948–65

(dollar figures in millions)

Year	Publicly Offered	Directly Placed	Total	Per Cent Directly Placed
1948	271	2,263	2,534	89
1949	459	1,493	1,952	76
1950	165	1,679	1,844	91
1951	458	2,502	2,960	85
1952	1,218	2,886	4,104	70
1953	1,539	2,250	3,789	59
1954	968	2,275	3,243	70
1955	1,622	2,326	3,948	59
1956	1,925	2,875	4,800	60
1957	2,078	2,630	4,708	56
1958	2,544	2,130	4,674	46
1959	1,150	2,233	3,383	66
1960	1,724	2,395	4,119	58
1961	2,252	3,442	5,694	60
1962	1,222	3,678	4,900	75
1963	1,855	4,872	6,727	72
1964	1,217	5,895	7,112	83
1965	2,942	6,685	9,627	69

Source: Securities and Exchange Commission. Figures by industrial class are available from the SEC only since 1948.

Public utility direct placements have grown less than industrial direct placements (Table 3). Since 1950, they have fluctuated between 21 per cent (1962) and 38 per cent (1965) of all public utility cash debt offerings, and have constituted, on the average, about 25 per cent of all corporate direct placements (Table 5).

Rail direct placements (excluding equipment financing) have been negligible both in dollar terms (Table 4) and relative to total corporate direct placements (Table 5).

TABLE 3

*Public Utilities: Total Debt Cash Issues, Publicly Offered
and Directly Placed, 1948–65*

(dollar figures in millions)

Year	Publicly Offered	Directly Placed	Total	Per Cent Directly Placed
1948	2,076	740	2,816	26
1949	1,518	957	2,475	39
1950	1,654	868	2,522	34
1951	1,580	821	2,401	34
1952	1,954	1,017	2,971	34
1953	2,020	971	2,991	32
1954	2,596	1,169	3,765	31
1955	1,969	960	2,929	33
1956	1,932	890	2,822	32
1957	3,697	1,209	4,906	25
1958	3,552	1,191	4,743	25
1959	2,255	1,377	3,632	38
1960	2,888	862	3,750	23
1961	2,326	1,229	3,555	35
1962	3,048	829	3,877	21
1963	2,482	1,237	3,719	33
1964	2,119	1,301	3,420	38
1965	2,369	1,444	3,813	38

Source: Securities and Exchange Commission. Figures by industrial class are available from the SEC only since 1948.

The proximate reasons for the growth of direct placements have been discussed extensively elsewhere [4] but some of the consequences of that growth are worth mentioning here.

1. Substantial competitive pressure has been put on investment

[4] See R. E. Corey, *Direct Placement of Corporate Securities,* Boston, 1951, pp. 51–68 and *passim.* See also A. B. Cohan, *Private Placements and Public Offerings: Market Shares Since 1935,* Chapel Hill, North Carolina, January 1961, pp. 15–24.

TABLE 4

Rails: Total Debt Cash Issues, Publicly Offered and Directly Placed, 1948–65

(dollar figures in millions)

Year	Publicly[a] Offered	Directly Placed	Total	Per Cent Directly Placed
1948	618	5	623	1
1949	458	2	460	b
1950	542	12	554	2
1951	326	4	330	1
1952	472	52	524	10
1953	296	6	302	2
1954	440	39	479	8
1955	527	15	542	3
1956	369	12	381	3
1957	344	0	344	0
1958	238	1	238	b
1959	151	22	174	13
1960	194	18	211	9
1961	128	52	180	29
1962	216	9	226	4
1963	381	49	431	11
1964	286	47	333	14
1965	259	22	281	8

Source: Securities and Exchange Commission. Figures by industrial class are available from the SEC only since 1948.

[a]Includes railway equipment trust certificates.

[b]Less than one-half of 1 per cent.

bankers, and the cost of flotation of publicly offered industrial and utility issues has declined sharply.[5]

2. Certain types of unconventional ventures have been able to

[5] The growth of direct placements was only partly responsible for this decline. See A. B. Cohan, *Cost of Flotation of Long Term Corporate Debt Since 1935*. Chapel Hill, North Carolina, 1961, pp. 87–89.

TABLE 5

Industrial, Utility, and Rail Debt Direct Placements as
Per Cent of Total Corporate Debt Directly Placed, 1948–65

Year	Industrials	Utilities	Rails	Total[a]
1948	75.2	24.6	0.2	100.0
1949	60.9	39.0	0.1	100.0
1950	65.6	33.9	0.5	100.0
1951	75.2	24.7	0.1	100.0
1952	73.0	25.7	1.3	100.0
1953	69.7	30.1	0.2	100.0
1954	65.3	33.6	1.1	100.0
1955	70.5	29.1	0.5	100.0
1956	76.1	23.6	0.3	100.0
1957	68.5	31.5	0	100.0
1958	64.1	35.9	0	100.0
1959	61.5	37.9	0.6	100.0
1960	73.1	26.3	0.5	100.0
1961	72.9	26.0	1.1	100.0
1962	81.4	18.4	0.2	100.0
1963	79.1	20.1	0.8	100.0
1964	81.4	18.0	0.6	100.0
1965	82.0	17.7	0.3	100.0
Average	73.7	25.8	0.5	100.0

[a]Due to rounding, will not always add to total.

obtain financing that would not have been so readily available, and might not have been available at all, elsewhere. The financial institutions are able to provide this "custom tailoring" service because they enter the market as ultimate purchasers (i.e., they are not wholesalers as are investment bankers), and they are free therefore to buy issues on the merits thereof, without regard to whatever fashions, traditions, or prejudices may dominate the *public* securities market.

3. Many small, relatively unknown firms, which would probably

have found the cost of a public offering prohibitive, have been able to obtain long-term debt financing at moderate cost.[6] The financial institutions are able to provide funds to such firms because they buy for their own portfolios and not, as do the investment bankers, for resale to the general public. An investment banker would only rarely be able to buy a small issue (say, $500,000) from a small, little-known company without making a high, perhaps a prohibitively high, charge to cover the cost required to sell such an issue to the public.[7]

Purposes of the Study

Although we know enough about direct placements to be conscious of the prominent place they have come to occupy in the market for corporate long-term funds, we have very little systematic information about them. This rather large subcontinent of the capital market is virtually unexplored.

In addition to the aggregate figures published by the Securities and Exchange Commission on total dollar volume, a few series have been published for 1951–58 on average (unadjusted) yields, dollar volume by industrial category, average size, and maturity. But all these series are annual and some of them are, unavoidably, inadequate conceptually; the yield series, for example, were constructed of raw, unadjusted data and, as a result, are far from being homogeneous through time.[8]

The primary purpose of this study, then, is to initiate the

[6] Bank term loans would be available to such firms for not more than five years. Direct placements are only rarely as short as five years.

[7] Between 1951 and 1958 the average size, annually, of industrial public offerings ranged between $28 million and $70 million. The average size of industrial direct placements ranged between $2 million and $3 million. See Chapter 6 for estimates of cost of flotation of small issues.

For further discussion of the pros and cons of direct placement, see Roscoe Steffen, "The Private Placement Exemption," *The University of Chicago Law Review,* Winter, 1963, p. 211, and A. B. Cohan, "Should Direct Placements be Registered?" *The North Carolina Law Review,* February 1965, p. 298.

[8] See *28th Annual Report of the Securities and Exchange Commission, 1962,* Table 3, Part 4; and A. B. Cohan, *Private Placements and Public Offerings,* pp. 15–24.

collection and analysis of systematic "relevant" data on direct placements by: (1) Constructing series on yields on direct placements which would be homogeneous through time; (2) constructing series on various other aspects of direct placements; (3) making selected comparisons between the characteristics of direct placements and those of public offerings.

Some Definitions

What is a direct placement? For the purposes of this study a direct placement is defined as a long-term corporate security, either debt or equity, sold for cash to a restricted number of institutional investors, without public offering.

The meaning of this definition will perhaps be clearer if the two essential distinctions between a direct placement and a public offering are made explicit. First, in a direct placement the corporate issuer and the (prospective ultimate) investors deal directly with each other, with or without the aid of an intermediary, in establishing the terms of a security issue.[9] In a public offering, on the other hand, the ultimate purchasers are a widely scattered multitude of individual investors and, although the issuer may attempt to sense their wishes, he does not negotiate terms with them. He either sets the terms himself and then throws the issue on the market, as in the case of a competitively bid utility issue, or he negotiates terms with an intermediate purchaser (in effect with a wholesaler), usually an investment banker.

Second, in a direct placement all the prospective ultimate purchasers must be "sophisticated," which in practice means that their number tends to be small. In a public offering, on the other hand, the prospective ultimate purchasers are in fact the entire public at large.

Issues which satisfy these criteria, i.e., which are negotiated directly with a *small number of sophisticated lenders,* are usually

---

[9] Intermediaries help the issuer in about half of all direct placements.

considered as "not involving any public offering" under Section 4
(1) of the Securities Act and, as such, are exempt from registration.[10]

The above definition excludes bank term loans and mortgages
on business property, and is therefore somewhat arbitrary.[11] Both
bank term loans and mortgages on business property are sold
directly to a limited number of sophisticated investors. Both provide
substantial amounts of long-term funds to business, and both are
regarded, at least by some issuers, as sources of funds alternative
to direct placement.[12]

The distinction between so-called direct placements, on the one
hand, and bank term loans and mortgages on business property
on the other, is sometimes made in terms of size and maturity:
term loans and mortgages on business property are usually small,
and the former rarely run over ten years and have an average
maturity in the neighborhood of five years. The distinction is sometimes made in terms of the business of the borrower: mortgages
on business property are made mostly to commercial rather than

[10] Prior to 1953, the Commission described direct placements as "offerings to a
single investor or a small number of investors, the offering being handled directly
by the company itself (i.e. the issuer) or by an investment banker. The bulk of
private (direct) placements are corporate securities exempt from registration under Section 4 (1) of the Securities Act of 1933. . . ." (Securities and Exchange
Commission, *Privately-Placed Securities—Cost of Flotation,* Washington, D.C.,
corrected printing, September 1952, p. 2). Since 1953, however, doubtless as a
result of the Supreme Court's decision in the Ralston Purina case, the Commission
has tended to refer to direct placements simply as "issues exempt under Section
4 (1) of the Securities Act—that is, issues not involving any public offering,"
without making clear what, in its view, constitutes a public offering. See 346
U.S. 119 (1953). The Supreme Court said: "An offering to those who are shown
to be able to fend for themselves is a transaction 'not involving any public offering' " and ". . . there is no warrant for superimposing a quantity limit on private
offerings as a matter of statutory interpretation. . . ."

[11] It also excludes, of course, loans made or equity issues bought by small
business investment corporations and small groups of individuals, etc.

[12] Financial officers of life insurance companies have been heard to say that
many of the business loans made through their mortgage departments could just
as well have been made through their securities departments. However, the survey
made by the Life Insurance Association of America for the Patman Committee
indicated that life insurance companies do not often make really "small" loans
through their securities departments. U.S. Congress, House Select Committee on
Small Business, "Problems of Small Business Financing," *Hearings,* 85th Congress,
1st Session, November 1957, Part I, pp. 142–170.

to industrial borrowers. It is sometimes made in terms of form: neither the business mortgage nor the bank term loan uses an indenture or a trustee; in the strict sense, therefore, neither is a "security." In addition, the terms of the typical direct placement agreement tend to go beyond the terms of the typical mortgage loan. Direct placements will often, for example, impose restrictions on working capital and the payment of dividends.[13]

The foregoing distinctions, although useful for some purposes, are obviously not essential. All three types of loans are long term and all are negotiated directly between the borrower and a limited number of lenders.

The distinction drawn in this study is simply a practical one. The study covers only those issues bought directly by the securities departments of life insurance companies and pension funds and by other nonbank financial institutions such as benevolent associations and mutual funds. Hence, it does *not* include business mortgages, except to the extent that loans which are in every respect mortgage loans may have been made by such securities departments. And it does not include bank term loans, except to the extent that banks may have taken the first few years of a longer loan, or otherwise participated in a loan with one or more insurance companies or pension funds.[14]

Public offerings are defined as issues of any size or maturity sold for cash, either directly by the issuer or by the issuer through an intermediary (such as an investment banker) to the public at

---

[13] For a discussion of these points, see Corey, *Direct Placements,* pp. 4, 116–117; and W. B. Hickman, *The Volume of Corporate Bond Financing,* p. 30. The distinction in terms of form is tending to become less important as, for example, the insurance companies seek (and find) simpler ways of doing things. For instance, many private placement agreements make no provision for a trustee.

[14] This is, in fact, the "definition" used in the trade and which underlies the SEC's series on the dollar volume of direct placements. That series is based to a large extent on data obtained from life insurance companies under the designation "securities issues." The SEC does not, of course, examine individual agreements, so that if a large loan closely resembling a mortgage happened to have been made, for one reason or another, by the securities department of a life insurance company, such a loan might well have been reported to the SEC under the designation "securities issues," and if so would have been included in the series referred to above.

large or to the issuer's own stockholders. Public offerings include both underwritten issues and those not underwritten. The latter include both those made without the assistance of an intermediary and those in which the intermediary acts on an agency or "best efforts" basis. With one or two relatively unimportant exceptions (e.g., issues which are sold intrastate), public offerings must be registered with the Securities and Exchange Commission. As indicated above, direct placements need not be so registered.

This study is occupied solely with *pure debt* corporate direct placements. A small portion of all direct placements are equities (Table 6). In addition, a small but increasing portion are debt issues with equity features—convertibility, warrants to purchase common stock, and so forth.

The term debt, as used here, includes debentures, notes, mortgage bonds and notes of whatever kind, collateral trust bonds or notes, notes secured by leases, and so forth—in short, every obligation which would be carried by the issuing company as a long-term liability. The term pure debt, as used here, includes all such debt issues except those with equity features.

To summarize: the phenomena studied are new pure debt issues of maturity longer than one year, bought directly from corporate borrowers by the securities departments of life insurance companies, pension funds, and various other nonbank financial institutions such as benevolent societies and mutual funds. Among these issues are surely some which are indistinguishable in substance, size, or form (or for that matter by any other test) from bank term loans and business mortgages.

The Sample

A very large percentage of all the pure debt corporate direct placements bought in the United States during the period under review were bought by one or some combination of about sixty organizations: fifty-odd life insurance companies, three or four benevolent associations, two or three large pension funds, and one large

TABLE 6

Direct Placements Sold in the United States, by Type of Security, 1935–65

(million dollars)

Year	Bonds and Notes	Equities[a]	Total	Equities as Per Cent of Total
1935	385	2	387	0.5
1936	369	4	373	1.1
1937	327	3	330	0.9
1938	691	1	692	0.1
1939	703	4	706	0.6
1940	758	7	765	0.9
1941	811	2	813	0.2
1942	411	9	420	2.1
1943	369	3	372	0.8
1944	778	9	787	1.1
1945	1,004	18	1,022	1.8
1946	1,863	54	1,917	2.8
1947	2,147	88	2,235	3.9
1948	3,008	79	3,087	2.6
1949	2,453	49	2,502	2.0
1950	2,560	120	2,680	4.5
1951	3,326	88	3,415	2.6
1952	3,957	45	4,002	1.1
1953	3,228	90	3,318	2.7
1954	3,484	185	3,668	5.0
1955	3,301	176	3,477	5.1
1956	3,777	109	3,886	2.8
1957	3,839	86	3,925	2.2
1958	3,320	169	3,490	4.8
1959	3,632	122	3,755	3.2
1960	3,275	221	3,497	6.3
1961	4,720	279	4,999	5.6
1962	4,529	113	4,643	2.4
1963	6,158	255	6,413	4.0
1964	7,243	261	7,504	3.5
1965	8,150	399	8,550	4.7

Source: Securities and Exchange Commission.

[a]Includes both common and preferred.

TABLE 7

Per Cent of Total Dollar Amount of Debt Direct
Placements Bought by Various Classes of Buyers,
Selected Years, 1947—55

	1947	1950	1953	1955
Life insurance companies	93.0	83.4	87.0	85.0
Other insurance companies	0.1	0.7	0.1	0.3
Banks	2.7	12.1	5.7	5.8
Eleemosynary institutions	2.5	0.5	0.4	1.2
Others[a]	0.4	2.5	5.5	6.0
Unknown	1.3	0.8	1.3	1.7
Total	100.0	100.0	100.0	100.0

Source: Securities and Exchange Commission

[a]Includes other corporations, pension and retirement funds, partnerships and individuals.

mutual fund.[15] The insurance companies and the benevolent associations had total assets, as of December 31, 1959, of $103.7 billion.

The sample of direct placements used in this study consists, in principle, of all the pure debt direct placements bought by twenty-three of the insurance companies and one large pension fund.[16] The twenty-three companies were selected (from a somewhat larger number of companies which had agreed to participate in the study) to approximate as closely as possible the size distribution of assets of the sixty-odd organizations mentioned above. The twenty-three insurance companies had total assets, as of December 31, 1959,

[15] Data prepared by the Securities and Exchange Commission suggest that by far the largest portion, in dollar terms, was taken by the life insurance companies. See Table 7.

[16] Every effort was made to collect data on all, but this effort was not always successful.

TABLE 8

*Distribution of Assets by Size Class, Total Life Insurance
Companies and Benevolent Associations, and Life Insurance
Companies Included in Sample, as of December 31, 1959*

Asset Size Class (million dollars)	Fifty-Three Life Insurance Companies and Three Benevolent Associations		Twenty-Three Life Insurance Companies Included in Sample		Coverage Ratio
	Million Dollars (1)	Per Cent[a] (2)	Million Dollars (2)	Per Cent[a] (4)	(Col. 4 ÷ Col. 2) (5)
100–500	5,725.2	5.5	1,937.4	2.6	.34
501–1,000	8,840.9	8.5	2,805.5	3.7	.32
1,001–2,500	16,395.0	15.8	12,322.3	16.2	.75
2,501–5,000	17,532.9	16.9	10,538.7	13.9	.60
5,001–10,000	22,429.4	21.6	15,505.9	20.4	.69
Over 10,000	32,809.5	31.6	32,809.5	43.2	1.00
Total	103,732.9	100.0	75,919.3	100.0	

[a]Due to rounding, will not necessarily add to total.

of $75.9 billion (Table 8).[17] Table 8 compares the size distribution of assets of the twenty-three companies with the size distribution of the sixty-odd organizations active in the direct placement market. This table indicates that the two distributions are very much alike in the middle but differ some in the tails; the sample companies include a smaller percentage of very small and a larger percentage of very large companies. This result suggested the possibility that the distribution of placements in the sample might not be representative.

[17] The fact that data were collected only at twenty-three life insurance companies (and one pension fund) does not mean that the other forty-odd organizations were not represented in the sample. The companies in the sample participated in the purchase of placements not only with each other but also with various other life insurance companies, the benevolent associations, the other pension funds, and the mutual fund. Some issues, however, had no chance to appear in the sample, namely, those which were wholly bought by one or more of the other forty-odd organizations.

TABLE 9

Industrials: Direct Placements, Average Yield and Average Size of Issue, Sample Compared with "Universe," Annually, 1951–65

Year	Sample		"Universe"	
	Yield (per cent)	Size (million $)	Yield (per cent)	Size (million $)
1951	3.95	15.3	3.84	6.4
1952	4.19	7.0	4.30	7.2
1953	4.59	4.2	4.43	5.6
1954	4.29	7.4	4.44	5.4
1955	4.41	4.1	4.35	5.7
1956	4.82	10.0	4.78	6.3
1957	5.45	9.1	5.21	5.7
1958	5.29	6.5	5.31	5.7
1959	5.77	4.9	5.58	4.3
1960	5.94	7.0	5.98	4.1
1961	5.76	5.6	5.76	5.4
1962	n.a.	n.a.	5.81	4.5
1963	n.a.	n.a.	5.65	6.0
1964	n.a.	n.a.	5.64	6.2
1965	n.a.	n.a.	5.67	5.7

An attempt to test this hypothesis was made by using the data on direct placements provided by the *Investment Dealers' Digest* (IDD). The IDD regularly publishes data on the dollar amount and the yield of virtually the whole "universe" of direct placements. These data were used to construct annual series on average yield and average size of issue for industrial, utility, and finance company placements separately.[18] Chart 5 and Tables 9, 10, and 11 compare the yield series with sample averages. On the whole, both sets of series are much the same, and yield, of course, is the best single test of homogeneity.

[18] The IDD does not date issues *within* the year and hence quarterly or monthly series could not be constructed.

Certain life insurance company officers have suggested to me that the IDD's coverage is not complete. But the IDD data were the only data available for the purpose at hand, inasmuch as the SEC does not publish information on individual placements.

TABLE 10

Public Utilities: Direct Placements, Average Yield and Average Size of Issue, Sample Compared with "Universe," Annually, 1951–65

	Sample		"Universe"	
	Yield (per cent)	Size (million $)	Yield (per cent)	Size (million $)
1951	3.71	2.9	3.59	4.0
1952	3.78	4.4	4.01	5.2
1953	4.12	9.0	4.15	8.8
1954	3.67	4.3	4.07	6.0
1955	3.86	3.8	4.01	4.0
1956	4.56	4.0	4.36	4.3
1957	5.27	5.5	5.13	4.9
1958	4.92	5.6	5.03	4.5
1959	5.31	9.2	5.34	5.3
1960	5.64	5.4	5.69	4.6
1961	5.26	4.9	5.37	4.6
1962	n.a.	n.a.	5.24	4.6
1963	n.a.	n.a.	5.07	5.6
1964	n.a.	n.a.	5.17	4.8
1965	n.a.	n.a.	5.11	4.2

Data were collected from the twenty-three companies and the pension fund on about 3,800 direct placements, of which about 2,300 were industrial, 900 were utility, and 600 were finance company placements. Of these, some 1,400 eventually turned out to be incomplete in some essential respect. Data collected by the IDD suggest that over the eleven years in question some 8,800 direct placements were negotiated. The effective sample used in this study, then, constitutes about 27 per cent by number of the underlying population.[19]

According to SEC figures, $39.9 billion of directly placed bonds and notes were "taken down" during the period 1951–61, of which

[19] *Investment Dealers' Digest, Corporate Financing Directory,* first half of 1961, p. 10. The SEC does not make available data on number of direct placements. The IDD figures include an indeterminate number of debt issues with equity features.

TABLE 11

Finance Companies: Direct Placements, Average Yield and Average Size of Issue, Sample Compared with "Universe," Annually, 1951–65

	Sample		"Universe"	
	Yield (per cent)	Size (million $)	Yield (per cent)	Size (million $)
1951	4.12	5.7	4.02	3.1
1952	4.74	6.7	4.57	2.5
1953	4.91	4.7	4.73	6.3
1954	4.16	13.6	4.54	6.5
1955	4.23	7.3	4.66	3.5
1956	4.78	7.0	4.68	5.9
1957	5.75	5.9	5.45	3.4
1958	5.45	2.5	5.45	3.5
1959	5.84	7.0	5.65	5.9
1960	6.09	7.6	6.04	5.9
1961	5.90	5.1	5.89	4.0
1962	n.a.	n.a.	5.72	5.2
1963	n.a.	n.a.	5.68	4.7
1964	n.a.	n.a.	5.48	5.7
1965	n.a.	n.a.	5.46	5.1

about $20.0 billion were taken down by industrial companies, $11.7 billion by utilities, and the remainder by finance and real estate companies and rails (rails accounted for only $219 million). The effective sample used in this study constitutes about 21 per cent by value of utilities placements and about 50 per cent by value of industrial, financial, and real estate placements—or about 44 per cent of all types taken together.

Summary of Findings

DETERMINANTS OF YIELD

The yields on the direct placements bought at any given time—on any given day or in any given week—vary widely from one another. They vary because borrowers vary and because the issues borrowers sell vary. Borrowers vary from one another in a good many ways: in size, capital structure, working capital, efficiency, and so forth. Issues also vary in a good many ways: in size, maturity, refundability, restrictive covenants, and so forth. This study has endeavored, first, to ascertain which characteristics of borrowers and of issues exert a perceptible influence on yield, and which do not—time held constant. Nineteen characteristics were tested for industrial, eighteen for utility, and seventeen for finance company placements. These are discussed in Chapter 2 and listed in Tables 12 and 13. Results are summarized below.

1. For industrials, the primary determinants of yield, in the order of their importance, were total pro-forma interest, size of company (as measured by total capital), earnings before interest and taxes, and size of issue. (See footnote 20 below.)

2. For utilities, the primary determinants were total pro-forma interest, size of company, average term, and earnings before interest and taxes.

3. For both classes of issues, variables such as type of security, industrial class, years nonrefundable, and maturity, while significant, did not have much impact on yield.

4. For finance company placements, the primary determinants of yield were size of issue, earnings, and type of security.

5. Growth in earnings, which had been expected to show strong significance for all three types of issues, showed none at all. The variability of earnings showed slight significance for finance company issues only.

6. The effect of duration (i.e., average term and maturity) on yield is not consistently in one direction: during some periods, higher yields were associated with shorter duration, and in other periods the reverse was the case. This was true for both industrials and utilities. In general, the direction of the effect of duration on yield appears to depend on expectations as to the future course of interest rates. When yields are expected to rise, longer duration tends to be associated with higher yields, and vice versa.

THE YIELD SERIES

Three types of series were constructed.

The first type simply represented average quarterly yields for 1951–61, unadjusted in any way, on all the issues in the sample. Separate series of this type were constructed for industrials, utilities, and finance companies.

The second, termed cross-classified yields, were also constructed quarterly for 1951–61. These series, which are based on the original observations, hold two of the most important variables approximately constant through time: times charges earned and size of company.[20] In effect, these series represent the changing cost, over time, of issues which are reasonably homogeneous over time. Separate series of this type were constructed for industrials and utilities only.

The third type, termed computed yields, and constructed quarterly for 1951–61, are series that hold *all* significant variables constant at their 1951–61 mean values. They are therefore, for all practical purposes, perfectly homogeneous through time. In effect, each of these series represents the changing cost over time of an issue of fixed characteristics. Separate series of this type were constructed for industrials, utilities, and finance companies.

Chart 1 compares the three computed series with each other and with long-term governments. Charts 2, 3, and 4 compare the computed series with the actuals for industrial, utility, and finance company placements, respectively.

Except for two or three erratic fluctuations in the industrial series at the outset of the period, all three series moved in much the same way. In addition, all conformed fairly closely to quarterly

---

[20] When *all* the significant variables were run simultaneously, times charges earned was broken into two separate variables: earnings before interest and taxes (EBIT) and total pro-forma interest. But, for the purpose of constructing the cross-classified series, EBIT and total pro-forma interest were combined into a measure of times pro-forma interest earned. See discussion of this matter on pp. 59ff.

CHART 1

Computed Yields on Industrial, Utility, and Finance Company Direct Placements Compared with Yields on Long-Term Governments, Quarterly, 1951–61

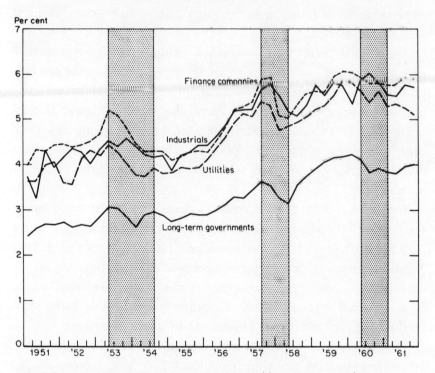

Shaded areas represent business contractions; white areas, expansions.
SOURCE: Tables 32, 48, 60; and *Federal Reserve Bulletin.*

turning points in business cycles and to the movements of long-term governments.

The utility series is lower than the industrial series in thirty-nine of forty-four quarters, despite the fact that the average industrial issue seems to be of substantially better "quality" than the average utility issue (the average industrial issue is larger and of shorter duration and is supported by higher average earnings and by much higher coverage of interest charges). The explanation of this anomaly is very likely to be found in the fact that lenders believe

CHART 2

*Industrials: Actual Average Yields and Computed Yields on Issue
of Fixed Characteristics, Quarterly, 1951–61*

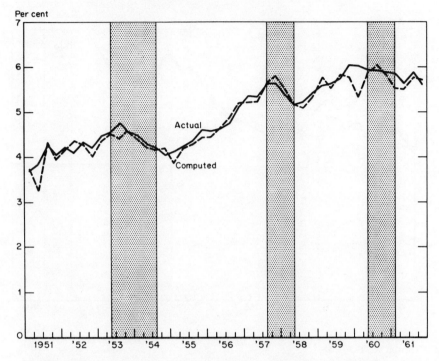

Shaded areas represent business contractions; white areas, expansions.
SOURCE: Table 32.

that utilities would fare better than industrials under conditions
of extreme adversity.

The quarterly differences between the actuals and the computed
yields range up to about seventy basis points for industrials, up to
about sixty basis points for utilities, and up to about 100 basis
points for finance companies. But on the whole, the actuals and
the computed series move in much the same way.[21] This could not,
of course, have been known in advance.

[21] This means that the "universe" series given in Chart 5 and Tables 9, 10,
and 11 probably represent fairly well the behavior of yields since 1961.

CHART 3

*Utilities: Actual Average Yields and Computed Yields on Issue
of Fixed Characteristics, Quarterly, 1951–61*

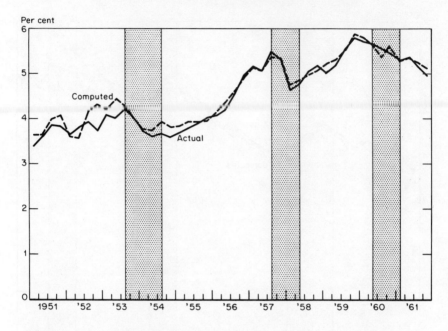

Shaded areas represent business contractions; white areas, expansions.
SOURCE: Table 48.

YIELDS ON DIRECT PLACEMENTS COMPARED WITH YIELDS
ON PUBLIC OFFERINGS

The findings suggest that yields on direct placements were higher,
on the average over the whole period, than yields on public offerings,
even after the latter were adjusted for cost of flotation. The
difference in favor of public offerings is not, however, constant
for all types of issues. For the smaller issues *alone,* the difference
appears to be negative for industrials (i.e., direct placements have
lower yields) and close to zero for utilities.[22] The explanation is,
very likely, that the direct placement market prefers higher-yielding
(lower-quality) issues and tends, therefore, to compete more

[22] This comparison was made for industrials and utilities only.

CHART 4

*Finance Companies: Actual Average Yields and Computed Yields
on Issue of Fixed Characteristics, Quarterly, 1951–61*

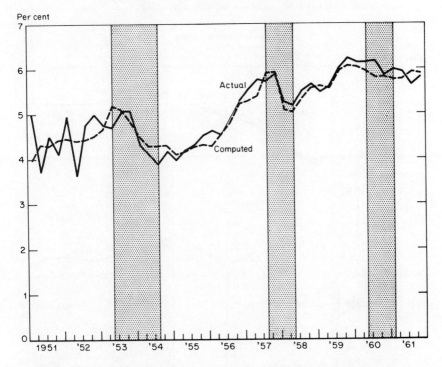

Shaded areas represent business contractions; white areas, expansions.
SOURCE: Table 60.

vigorously with the public market for such issues. This means that yields on lower-quality issues tend to be lower in the direct placement market than in the public market. It means also, conversely, that the direct placement market, especially when money is "tight," is little interested in the lower-yielding (higher-quality) issues and tends therefore to compete less vigorously with the public market for such issues. Hence, yields on such issues tend to be lower in the public market than in the direct placement market.[23]

---

[23] Of course, in trying to decide whether to sell an issue publicly or directly, issuers take *all* things into account, not just price. A small issuer may place a

CHART 5

Industrial, Utility, and Finance Company Direct Placements:
Average Yields in Sample, Annually, 1951–61, and Average
"Universe" Yields, Annually, 1951–65

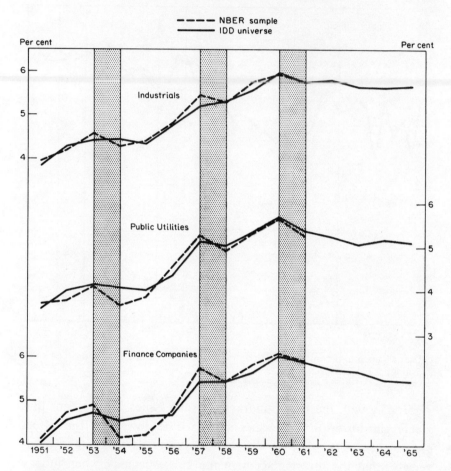

Shaded areas represent business contractions; white areas, expansions.
SOURCE: Tables 9, 10, and 11.

DISTRIBUTION OF DIRECT PLACEMENTS BY CLASS

In order to construct the "cross-classified" series described above, it became necessary to construct classes for direct placements. These classes were used to compare the distribution of direct placements by class with the distribution of public offerings by class. The principal finding was that the average "quality" of public offerings is probably substantially higher than the average "quality" of direct placements—virtually all public offerings fell in classes 1 through 4, whereas 49.5 per cent of industrial and 31.0 per cent of utility direct placements fell in those classes.[24] As indicated above, these classes were based on a combination of two variables: size of company and times pro-forma interest earned.

CHARACTERISTICS OF DIRECT PLACEMENTS

With respect to the individual characteristics of direct placements, three facts stand out: (1) the size and earnings variables increased, on the average, from the first half of the period to the second half; (2) although earnings rose, pro-forma interest rose more rapidly and hence times pro-forma interest earned declined; (3) the other variables—maturity, average term, lien position, and years nonrefundable—remained much the same.

high value on wide distribution of an issue and may therefore be willing to pay a premium to the public market to obtain it. A larger issuer, on the other hand, may want a firm commitment quickly and, in order to obtain it, may be willing to pay a premium to the direct placement market. See Chapter 6, below.

[24] These comparisons were made for industrials and utilities only.

2

STATISTICAL TECHNIQUES, PROBLEMS OF MEASUREMENT, VARIABLES

As indicated in Chapter 1, the primary purpose of this study has been to construct series on yields on direct placements which would be comparable through time—series, that is, which would represent the behavior through time of yields on reasonably homogeneous instruments. This problem is identical in principle to that of comparing the prices of automobiles between two points in time. If, for such purpose, we simply used average prices, fluctuations would doubtless occur simply because an increase had occurred, from one period to another, in the number of "high-quality" (or "low-quality") cars sold, or because the meaning of high-quality (or low-quality) had itself changed.

In brief, some way had to be found of isolating those characteristics of direct placements which tended during the period to be associated significantly with variations in yield, so that, as a first approximation, those characteristics could be held constant through time. If this were not done, the series would not measure mere changes in the price of a stable commodity; they would measure also intrinsic changes in the commodity itself.

But series which hold characteristics constant will be homogeneous with respect to *quality* through time only if the weight attached to each characteristic does not change through time—or if such changes as do occur are offsetting.

In other words, the term "quality" is usually taken to mean the condition of certain ratios underlying an issue (e.g., times charges earned). It should, rather, be taken to mean the ex ante probability that the promise made by the borrower will be kept in full. Consider two loans making the identical promise, containing identical auxiliary terms, and resting on identical underlying ratios—but issued at two different moments of time. Clearly, if risk preferences and the general level of rates are held constant, any difference between the yields on the two loans must reflect a difference in ex ante quality, i.e., a difference at the two moments of time in the meaning of the underlying ratios. In short, the underlying ratios on which a loan rests are not themselves identical with quality. They are merely part of the ingredients out of which estimates of quality, half objective, half subjective, are made.

This is not just a pedantic point. In the mid-thirties, no industrial bond which had earned charges less than twenty times was classified as Aaa. Where did this magic figure come from? Obviously, in the judgment of the rating agencies the chances were close to zero that a depression would occur of such severity that the company in question would be unable to meet its charges. It is obvious also that virtually no one today would attach the same probability to the occurrence of a great depression as he would have thirty years ago. It follows that the probability of repayment (i.e., the quality) which would be attached now to a given set of underlying ratios would be higher than the probability which would have been attached to those ratios thirty or twenty or perhaps even ten years ago. It follows further that, if we merely held underlying ratios constant, the resulting series might show "drift" simply because the meaning of the ratios, in terms of quality, had changed.

The foregoing discussion means that procedures were required here which would (1) identify those characteristics of direct placements which were relevant during the period to variations in yield; and (2) assign weights to each such characteristic in a way that would enable us to judge whether those weights changed systematically during the period.

Cross-section multiple regression responded to these requirements better than any other available technique and therefore has been used here.

Ideally, strict cross sections of time should be used, but unfortunately the total number of observations was relatively small; indeed, on many days or even in many months during the period, the number of observations available would not have appreciably exceeded the number of variables to be taken into account. This problem has been dealt with here by the use of a half year (or a quarter, depending on degrees of freedom) as the "regression unit," and by the inclusion of commitment date as a variable—so as to eliminate some of the variation with respect to time within each half year (or quarter).

The Variables

Every effort has been made to include within our original perspective every variable which might conceivably have some bearing on yield.

The dependent variable, yield, is defined as yield at commitment date to maturity. Inasmuch as most placements are bought at par, this is usually simply the coupon. The yield on an issue bought at a premium or a discount is defined as the rate which equates the sum of expected cash inflows (interest plus amortization) to the amount received by the borrowing company.[1]

In addition to the yield it offers, a debt instrument has four primary aspects, each of which has been presumed, at the outset, to be relevant to variations in yield:

1. The promise. This is represented by the stipulated agreement to repay a specified amount of principal plus a specified amount of interest at specified times.

2. The quality of the promise. This is, presumably, some estimate

---

[1] A portion of all direct placements are what is known in the trade as "roll-overs." A roll-over is a loan which combines an outstanding balance on an old loan (by the same lender) with a new loan at a rate which is an average of that on the old and new loans. In almost every case, the final maturity is extended beyond the maturity of the old loan and amortization is recalculated. Loans of this type have not been included in the study primarily because no satisfactory method could be found to calculate the yield on net new funds.

(usually implicit) of the probability that the promise will be kept in full.

3. The security. This is the "cushion" likely to be available to the lender in the event that earnings fall temporarily or default occurs.

4. The auxiliary terms. These are represented by those terms which are not part of the promise and without bearing on the quality thereof or on the "cushion," e.g., call provisions and restrictive covenants other than those designed to improve the quality of the promise.

THE PROMISE

The following variables (represented by "X" designations) are aspects of the promise itself.

Average term (X_3) is simply the weighted average length of the loan. Any loan requiring amortization prior to maturity may be considered to be a series of loans. Thus, a $10,000 loan for ten years, required to be amortized at the rate of $1,000 a year, is really ten separate loans of $1,000 each for periods of one to ten years, i.e., $1,000 is being loaned for one year, $1,000 for two years, and so forth. The average term of the loan is then simply

$$\frac{\Sigma a_i t_i}{\Sigma a_i}$$

where $a_i \ldots a_n$ = the amount amortized annually and $t_i \ldots t_n$, the number of years for which each such amount, a_i, has been outstanding. The sum of $a_i \ldots a_n$ is, of course, the original amount of the loan. The average term of a loan thus represents the average length of time each dollar of the original loan was expected, at issue, to be outstanding.

Maturity (X_{13}) is the expected number of years to final maturity, i.e., the year in which the last payment on principal is expected to be made minus the year in which the loan was negotiated. This variable simply distinguishes between issues of the same average term but different final maturities.

Size of issue (X_8) is the total number of gross dollars received by the borrower. Cost of flotation, if any, has not been deducted.

Average size of issue (X_{16}) is the average amount expected to be outstanding per year during the life of the loan, calculated in a manner analogous to that of average term.[2]

QUALITY OF PROMISE

The "quality" of an issue is here assumed to be related to two broad classes of variables: (1) those which measure the ratio of the expected value of earnings before interest and taxes (EBIT) to pro-forma interest and (2) those which measure growth in and the variability of that ratio.

Times charges earned (X_4) is the ratio of earnings before interest and taxes (EBIT) to pro-forma interest. In general, lenders "look at" a five-year weighted average figure, EBIT, averaged over the immediately preceding five-year period, divided by pro-forma interest.

Earnings are stated in the accounting sense. They are sometimes adjusted (and sometimes not, depending on what the lending institution may have done) for items of income or expense, or both, which were expected to be nonrecurring. By and large, lenders tend to adjust earnings only for large nonrecurring items, i.e., those which are likely to have a noticeable effect on the size of the times-charges-earned ratio.

Interest is pro-forma total interest. Practice in this regard varies widely among lenders. Some include pro-forma interest expected to be payable on account of short-term bank borrowing and other short-term liabilities. Some use actual rather than pro-forma interest on the grounds that the latter will be "unfair" to growing companies. Happily, however, the basic data were always available and we were able to use a uniform standard of our own choosing.

[2] The numerator is the same in both cases but the denominators are different. In the calculation of average term, the denominator is the amount of the issue; in the calculation of average size, the denominator is the maturity of the issue.

Total pro-forma interest seemed a more reasonable choice than either pro-forma long-term interest or actual interest paid (whether total or merely long-term), especially given the fact that growth was to be taken into account in other ways.[3]

The ratio of EBIT to pro-forma interest, of course, tells the lender how many dollars of EBIT will be available to pay each dollar of expected charges, on the assumption that earnings in the future will be no worse than they have been in the immediate past. On the same assumption, the ratio is also a rough, indirect measure of the ability of the company to repay principal out of earnings. For example, on a 5 per cent, twenty-year loan, to be amortized in equal annual instalments, two times pro-forma interest (before taxes) would be equal to one instalment on the loan.[4] Thus, a times-charges-earned ratio of three would mean that the borrower's average earnings over the past five years would just be sufficient to pay interest plus amortization due in the first year. In a few cases, data on earnings were not available five years back. No issues were included however, unless three years were available.

Dispersion of EBIT (X_{17}). Two companies with the same average times-charges-earned ratio may present different degrees of risk because of differences in dispersion about those averages. In order to take variation of this sort into account, the standard deviation of EBIT was calculated (around trend) for each issue, and divided by the mean thereof.

Growth of EBIT (X_9). Three companies may have the same average times-charges-earned ratios, with the same dispersion, but represent, nevertheless, different degrees of risk: earnings in one case may be stable; in the second, growing; and in the third, declining. In order to take account of variation in this respect, least-squares trends were fitted to EBIT. The absolute amount of the trend was divided by the five-year mean of EBIT in order to put all trends on a comparable basis.

[3] In general, depreciation is left out of account in calculating the ratio.
[4] Assuming an approximate 50 per cent tax rate.

SECURITY

Lenders do not ask merely what, in any given case, the relative probability of repayment is—assuming the continuation of the conditions prevailing during the preceding five years. They ask also: (1) what would happen to any given loan if a recession occurred and (2) what recourse would be available if such a loan did, in fact, default?

In an attempt to answer these questions, lenders look primarily at the ratio of working capital to long-term debt, the ratio of long-term debt to total capital, and the lien position of the particular security.

The ratio of working capital to long-term debt (X_{14}). What does this ratio mean? Presumably, in a period of business recession, if sales declined, working capital would "run off" into cash and become available for repayment of long-term debt; i.e., inventory and receivables (on the asset side) would undergo a net decline, the addition to receivables would be less than collections (unless the decline in business activity affected the ability of customers to repay), and inventory would be used up faster than it was replaced.

Thus, a company which has a sizeable cushion of working capital relative to long-term debt would probably be able to service that debt for some time, even if sales declined, or perhaps pay it off entirely. Working capital, then, is a rough measure of recession-liquidity, and the ratio of working capital to long-term debt is a measure of recession-liquidity per dollar of long-term debt.

For the present purpose, the relevant ratio has been taken to be that of pro-forma working capital to pro-forma long-term debt. For finance companies, the following variables were used: the ratio of cash plus net receivables to total debt (X_{22}), the ratio of net receivables to EBIT (X_{20}), trend in the latter ratio (X_{21}) and the standard deviation around that trend (X_{25}). The ratio of net receivables to EBIT was a proxy for the ratio of net receivables to volume of business on which data were not available over a sufficiently large number of issues. The ratio of net receivables to volume of business is a measure of the average term of net receivables. A low ratio tends to indicate that receivables are turning rapidly.

The ratio of long-term debt to total capital (X_{15}). Lenders are also interested in what their position is likely to be if the company defaults and its creditors should be obliged to foreclose. A rough measure of this is provided by the ratio of total debt to net tangible assets.[5] This ratio measures the "cushion" which would be available to the company's creditors in the event of liquidation. For example, if the ratio is .50, total assets could be sold at 50 per cent of their respective book values and still leave sufficient funds to pay off all debt in full. As an index of this "cushion," the ratio of pro-forma long-term debt to total pro-forma capitalization has been used.[6] For finance companies, the ratio of net worth to senior and equal long-term debt was used (X_{24}).

Type of lien (X_5). Lenders are also interested in the position they will occupy should foreclosure become necessary. All loans have therefore been classified in terms of lien position. The assumption has been made that any loan secured by specific property (real or other) or specific income (i.e., rents) will carry a lower yield (all else being equal) than an unsecured loan. All loans have been put into one or another of the following classes: (1) first lien on specific property; (2) other lien on specific property, secured by securities or by a lease; (3) senior debenture or note; and (4) subordinated debenture or note.

AUXILIARY TERMS

Years nonrefundable (X_7) is the only variable in this category which has been taken into account. Call premia were left out primarily because, in most cases, they are fixed after yield has been

---

[5] Alternative measures would be total debt divided by total tangible assets and long-term debt divided by tangible net worth.

[6] The sum of net worth and pro-forma long-term debt. Data on total debt were not available on a sufficiently large number of issues.

determined and are the same as or not materially different from the coupon on the issue.

MISCELLANEOUS VARIABLES

Certain other variables which, on the surface, seem to add little if anything to those discussed above, have also been taken into account. These variables bear more on the issuer than on the issue itself, its quality or underlying security. They have been taken into account because lenders indicated that their "attitude" toward an issue could be substantially affected by them.

Size of company. In general, lenders feel more comfortable about a loan made to a large company than about one made to a small company. Therefore, other things being equal, yields on loans to large companies will tend to be less than yields on loans to small companies. Three measures of size have been used: a *five-year average of EBIT* (X_{12}), a five-year average of *sales* (X_{19}), and *total-pro-forma capitalization* (X_2).

Ratio of EBIT to sales (X_{10}, X_{11}, X_{18}). This ratio has been included as a test of efficiency. If two companies, identical in every other respect, differ in this respect, the presumption is that the company with the higher average ratio of EBIT to sales would be able to borrow at lower cost. If the two companies were identical also in terms of their *average* ratios, the presumption is that the company whose ratio showed the larger trend and/or the smaller standard deviation would be able to borrow at lower cost. Hence the ratio itself (averaged over the five-year period immediately preceding commitment date), the coefficient of variation of that average, and trend have all been taken into account. For finance companies, the ratio of EBIT to net worth (X_{23}) was used.

Industrial Classification (X_6). All issues have been classified by type of business of the borrower. Two classifications have been used for industrials—durable and nondurable; three for finance companies—sales finance, personal loan, and both; and five for utilities—electric and telephone, gas pipelines, water and gas distribution, urban transport, and other.

TABLE 12

Identification Number and Description of All Variables Tested

X_1	A time variable[a]
X_2	Total pro-forma capitalization
X_3	Average term
X_4	Times pro-forma interest earned
X_{4r}	Total pro-forma interest
X_5	Type of security
X_6	Industrial class
X_7	Years nonrefundable
X_8	Size of issue
X_9	Relative trend in EBIT (earnings before interest and taxes)
X_{10}	Relative trend in ratio of EBIT to sales
X_{11}	Coefficient of variation in ratio of EBIT to sales
X_{12}	EBIT
X_{13}	Maturity
X_{14}	Ratio of working capital to pro-forma long-term debt
X_{15}	Ratio of pro-forma long-term debt to pro-forma total capitalization
X_{16}	Average size of issue
X_{17}	Coefficient of variation of EBIT
X_{18}	Ratio of EBIT to sales
X_{19}	Sales
X_{20}	Ratio of net receivables to EBIT
X_{21}	Ratio of net receivables to EBIT, trend
X_{22}	Ratio of cash plus net receivables to total debt
X_{23}	Ratio of EBIT to net worth
X_{24}	Ratio of net worth to senior and equal pro-forma long-term debt
X_{25}	Ratio of net receivables to EBIT, σ around trend

[a]Month of quarter for industrials, quarter or half-year for utilities, and the yield on Aaa corporates for finance companies.

TABLE 13

Variables Tested for Each Class of Issue

	Industrials	Utilities	Finance Companies
X_1	x	x	x
X_2	x	x	x
X_3	x	x	x
X_4	x	x	x
X_{4r}	x	x	—
X_5	x	x	x
X_6	x	x	x
X_7	x	x	—
X_8	x	x	x
X_9	x	x	x
X_{10}	x	x	—
X_{11}	x	x	—
X_{12}	x	x	x
X_{13}	x	x	x
X_{14}	x	—	—
X_{15}	x	x	—
X_{16}	x	x	—
X_{17}	x	x	x
X_{18}	x	x	—
X_{19}	x	x	—
X_{20}	—	—	x
X_{21}	—	—	x
X_{22}	—	—	x
X_{23}	—	—	x
X_{24}	—	—	x
X_{25}	—	—	x

Table 12 lists, by identification number, all the variables tested. Table 13 indicates which of the variables discussed above were tested for each of the three classes of issues.[7]

[7] It goes without saying that some variables which just might have some bearing on yield have not been included in the analysis. Depreciation charges, for example, have nowhere been taken into account nor have so-called restrictive covenants, i.e., restrictions on dividend payments, on the sale of assets or on the issuance of equal or prior debt, and so forth. Depreciation charges have not been taken into account largely because data were not uniformly available. Restrictive covenants have not been taken into account largely because they could not be satisfactorily quantified.

3

YIELDS ON INDUSTRIALS

This chapter, the end product of which consists of two sets of series on yields on industrial direct placements, has three parts:

The first part describes the preliminary tests made of the variables checked in column 1 of Table 13. This part responds to the following question: How much of the variation in yields on direct placements, time held constant, do those variables together explain?

The second part describes the procedures used to identify the *significant* variables—those variables, that is, which can be said to be the determinants of yields on industrials, time held constant, and to rank them in order of importance. This part responds to the question: Which of the variables are statistically significant and, of these, which are really important and which are of slight importance, time held constant?

The last part of the chapter presents the various series on yields on industrials and describes the procedures used to construct them.

Summary of Procedure

Much of this chapter is technical and will probably not be of interest to the general reader. But for him, if he feels venturesome, and for others perhaps as well, a brief guide to the procedures used and their meaning may be helpful.

In general, two types of series have been constructed [1]—"cross-classified" series and "computed" series. The cross-classified series hold constant through time just two characteristics (variables), albeit two of the most important—size of issuer (as measured by

[1] In addition to simple quarterly averages, of the actual yields in the sample.

total pro-forma capital) and times pro-forma interest earned (coverage). These series represent the changing cost of various classes of direct placements, each of which is roughly homogeneous, with respect to these two variables, through time.

The computed series, on the other hand, hold *all* the relevant variables of an issue constant over time, and therefore represent the changing cost of various classes of direct placements, each of which is, for practical purposes, perfectly homogeneous through time. These series, that is, hold not only size of issuer and coverage constant but also eight other variables which, the analysis suggests, are capable of having some effect on yield. Each computed series is, thus, analogous to a cost of living index based on a rigidly fixed basket of commodities. Each measures the changing cost through time of a direct placement of specified characteristics.

In order to construct the computed series, all the variables capable of influencing yield had to be identified; in order to construct the cross-classified series, the most important variables had to be selected from among all the relevant variables.

The first step toward the accomplishment of these two objectives was to subject the eighteen substantive variables checked in column 1 of Table 13 to a five-step statistical procedure. Each variable was tested to determine whether it contributed anything to our understanding of yield, all other variables held constant. For this purpose, multiple regression techniques were used. Multiple regression is the statistical counterpart of the economists' "other things being equal." It enabled us to observe, first, whether some given variable was capable of affecting yield, all other variables held constant, and, if so, to measure that effect on a percentage scale.

Table 14, column 1, lists the substantive variables which survived the foregoing sifting process. Column 2 gives, for each such variable, the number which measures the size of the effect of the given variable on yield. Each of these numbers (regression coefficients) can be interpreted as an estimate of the percentage effect on yield when the variable with which it is associated is varied by 1 per cent. The sign of the regression coefficient indicates the direction

TABLE 14

Industrials: Significant Variables, Their Regression Coefficients and Percentage Impact on Yield

	Variable	Regression Coefficient	Percentage Impact on Yield[a]
X_2	Total pro-forma capital	-.0475	9
X_3	Average term (years)	-.0228	1
X_{4r}	Pro-forma interest	+.0683	12
X_5	Type of security	-.0232	2
X_6	Industrial class	-.0178	1
X_7	Years nonrefundable	+.0010	1
X_8	Size of issue	-.0195	3
X_{12}	Earnings before interest and taxes	-.0322	6
X_{13}	Maturity (years)	-.0212	1
X_{15}	Dollars of long-term debt per dollar of total capital	-.0349	2

[a]See text for explanation.

of effect. Thus, on the average over the sample, when EBIT (X_{12}), was 1 per cent higher, yield was lower by 322/10,000 of 1 per cent. When maturity (X_{13}) was longer by 1 per cent, yield was lower by 212/10,000 of 1 per cent—and so forth for each of the other regression coefficients.

The regression coefficients given in Table 14 are averages over the whole eleven-year period, 1951–61. In addition to these eleven-year averages, separate regression coefficients were obtained for each of the forty-four calendar quarters during the period. These quarterly coefficients are given in Appendix D.

In the next step, the total impact of each variable was assessed. Total impact is a combined measure which takes account of two things—the variability of each variable and the importance of that variability as measured by the appropriate regression coefficient. The regression coefficients alone tell us how much yield will vary with each 1 per cent change in each variable. But some variables vary little and others much. Thus, for example, size and earnings vary from a few hundred thousand dollars to several hundred million dollars, or by a multiple of perhaps a thousand. Maturities, on the other hand, range from eight or nine to twenty-five years, or by a multiple of about three.

Column 3 of Table 14 provides a combined estimate of total impact for each variable and indicates that, taking both variability and the importance of that variability into account, X_2, X_{4r}, and X_{12} have the most impact on yield.

With these findings in hand, the cross-classified series were constructed. The variables X_{4r} and X_{12} were combined into a single variable—coverage—and a trade-off factor was found between it and X_2. Two issues with different coverage ratios and sold by companies of different size were considered to represent approximately equivalent "quality" if the two variables, adjusted for the trade-off between them, for the first issue, were equal to the same two variables, similarly adjusted, for the second issue. This, of course, is just a roundabout way of saying that an issue sold by a large company with a low coverage ratio may be equivalent in quality to an issue sold by a small company with a high coverage ratio. The technical problem, which is discussed in detail below, lay in estimating the trade-off factor, in the above sense, between size of issuer and coverage. The factor actually used was tested on public offerings and found to conform fairly well to that implicit in agency ratings (see Appendix C). After the trade-off factor was ascertained, three classes were established and the actual observations deposited in them. Average yields within each class were computed quarterly. (The resulting series are given in Table 28 and in Chart 7.)

A *composite* cross-classified series, quarterly, was then obtained by averaging the three series across each quarter. This series is given in Table 28 and Chart 7, where it is compared with yields on FHA mortgages and long-term governments. It is compared with yields on Moody's new issues (Baa and A) in Chart 9.

Computed series were then obtained as follows: first, average values over the whole period for each variable for *each* of the above three classes were computed.[2] In other words, an average value for X_2 (total pro-forma capital) was obtained for class I by averaging over X_2 for all issues falling in class I over the entire eleven-year period. The same was done for each of the other nine variables. The same procedure was then followed for classes II and III (see Table 29). These values were then inserted into each of the forty-four quarterly regression equations described above, and yields calculated quarterly for each class. The three computed series will be found in Table 30 and in Chart 11, where they are compared with their cross-classified counterparts.

Finally, a computed composite series was obtained by using, for each variable, its average value over all observations for the year 1956. For example, the value used for X_2 was an average over X_2 for all the direct placements sold in the calendar year 1956, and so forth for each other variable. These values are given in Table 31.[3] The computed composite series itself is given in Table 32 and Chart 12 where it is compared with its cross-classified counterpart.

The rest of this chapter describes procedure in detail.

The Preliminary Tests

As indicated in Chapter 2, discussion with life insurance company financial managers had suggested that most of the variation in yield, time held constant, could be explained by some combination of the eighteen substantive variables checked in column 1 of Table 13.

In order to form a judgment regarding the shape of the function relating the foregoing variables to yield, scatter diagrams were

---

[2] That is, the three classes used to construct the cross-classified series.

[3] They are virtually identical to the average values for each variable over the entire period.

drawn for six quarters fairly well distributed through the period.[4] These quarters were chosen because, within each, the level of yields on outstandings had been reasonably stable and, therefore, each such quarter could be regarded as a reasonably close approximation to a strict cross section of time.[5]

The scatter diagrams showed yield on each variable for each of these six quarters. Six diagrams were thus obtained for yield on total pro-forma capitalization, yield on average term, yield on times pro-forma interest earned, and so forth. Examination of these diagrams strongly suggested that yield varied proportionately with the following thirteen variables: [6] total pro-forma capitalization, average term, times pro-forma interest earned, size of issue, the coefficient of variation of the ratio of EBIT to sales, EBIT, maturity, the ratio of pro-forma working capital to pro-forma long-term debt, ratio of pro-forma long-term debt to pro-forma total capitalization, average size of issue, the coefficient of variation of EBIT, the ratio of EBIT to sales, and sales itself. Logarithms were therefore used for these thirteen variables. Natural numbers were indicated for the remaining five variables.[7] The preliminary hypothesis then was of the form: $\text{Log } Y = a + b_1 \text{ Log } X_1 + b_2 X_2 + \ldots$, where Y is yield; X_1 represents the thirteen variables for which logarithms were used, and X_2 represents the five variables for which natural numbers were used.

Six regressions were then run on this function—one for each of the six quarters for which the scatter diagrams had been drawn. The results of these six regressions are given in Table 15. All showed high R^2's and highly significant F's.[8] For these six quarters,

---

[4] First quarter of 1951, second quarter of 1952, fourth quarter of 1954, fourth quarter of 1955, third quarter of 1956, and first quarter of 1961.

[5] This procedure assumed, of course, that if the level of yields on outstandings were reasonably stable the level of yields on direct placements would have been reasonably stable also.

[6] That is, when the given variable varied by some specified (constant) percentage, yield would also vary by some specified (constant) percentage.

[7] Logarithms could not, of course, be used for the trend variables inasmuch as, in many cases, trend was negative.

[8] The symbol R^2 refers to the proportion of the variation in yield explained by the independent variables; F is a test of the significance of the amount of

TABLE 15

Industrials: Fourteen Regressions, Yield on Eighteen Variables,
R^2, *F, Probability of F, Degrees of Freedom,*
Selected Quarters, 1951–61

Quarter and Year	R^2	F	$P_{F\lessgtr}$	Degrees of Freedom
1/1951[a]	.834	6.69	.01	24
2/1951	.852	7.05	.01	22
1/1952[a]	.810	5.22	.01	22
2/1952	.838	4.60	.01	16
1/1954	.919	10.78	.01	17
2/1954	.792	4.64	.01	22
4/1954[a]	.902	7.66	.01	15
2/1955	.849	4.70	.01	15
4/1955[a]	.850	4.39	.01	14
2/1956	.738	2.66	.05	17
3/1956[a]	.696	2.54	.05	20
4/1956	.683	2.16	.05	18
1/1961[a]	.857	5.34	.01	16
2/1961	.727	2.95	.05	20

[a] Six original regressions.

then, the preliminary hypothesis was, in fact, explaining a high percentage of variation in yield.

Eight additional regressions were then run in order to see how the hypothesis would behave under circumstances which seemed to be somewhat less favorable—i.e., in quarters in which some movement of yield on outstandings had, in fact, occurred. The results of these additional eight regressions are also given in Table 15. The R^2's ranged from .68 for the fourth quarter of 1956 to .92

variation being explained by the independent variables; P_F is the probability, on the basis of chance alone, of obtaining an F as high as that actually obtained.

for the first quarter of 1954. Of the fourteen R^2's taken together, two were .90 or better, nine were .80 or better and all but two were .72 or better.

These results were taken to mean that the preliminary hypothesis was explaining a satisfactory percentage of variation in yield (especially because time could not be held absolutely constant) and that therefore no substantial purpose was to be served by adding variables or experimenting with other forms of function.[9]

The Significant Variables

This part of the chapter is concerned with the question: Which of the foregoing variables had a measurable effect on yield more or less consistently through the period?

The procedure followed was, first, to choose twenty-two cross sections for each of the twenty-two half years, 1951–61. Twenty-two was decided upon rather than eleven or forty-four, or some other number, because twenty-two represented the "optimum" between degrees of freedom, on the one hand, and number of cross sections on the other.[10] Had more than twenty-two cross sections been chosen (the most likely larger number was forty-four, one for each quarter), degrees of freedom would have been negative in some periods. On the other hand, had fewer than twenty-two been chosen (the most likely smaller number was eleven, one for each year), degrees of freedom would have been larger and the cross section wider than seemed necessary.

Simple correlations were then obtained among all the variables, both dependent and independent (Y on X_1 through X_{19}) for *each* cross section. Thus, twenty-two simple correlation coefficients were obtained for Y on X_1, twenty-two for Y on X_2, and so forth. Twenty-two simple correlation coefficients were also obtained for

[9] Residuals were, for the most part, approximately normally distributed although a somewhat better fit would probably have been obtained in four of the fourteen quarters had the squared logarithms of some variables been used. These four quarters were 1/1951, 2/1952, 1/1954, 2/1954.

[10] In the judgment of the author.

TABLE 16

Industrials: *Weighted Average Correlation Coefficients, Y on Each X and Each X on Each Other Y, 1951–61*

	Y	X_2	X_3	X_4	X_5	X_6	X_7	X_8	X_9	X_{10}	X_{11}	X_{12}	X_{13}	X_{14}	X_{15}	X_{16}	X_{17}	X_{18}	X_{19}
Y	1.00																		
X_2	−.59 (0)	1.00																	
X_3	−.47 (0)	+.61 (22)	1.00																
X_4	−.33 (1)	+.13 (16)	+.05 (13)	1.00															
X_5	−.22 (4)	−.03 (11)	+.03 (13)	+.06 (13)	1.00														
X_6	−.07 (7)	+.04 (11)	+.07 (12)	−.04 (7)	−.09 (5)	1.00													
X_7	−.14 (4)	−.41 (22)	+.40 (22)	−.01 (10)	.01 (14)	−.05 (6)	1.00												
X_8	−.54 (0)	+.81 (22)	+.63 (22)	−.06 (8)	+.14 (16)	−.04 (6)	+.28 (21)	1.00											
X_9	−.07 (5)	−.04 (7)	−.03 (9)	+.14 (18)	−.02 (8)	+.05 (11)	−.07 (6)	−.03 (9)	1.00										
X_{10}	−.04 (9)	−.01 (12)	−.02 (10)	+.11 (18)	−.03 (8)	−.03 (9)	−.04 (8)	−.04 (10)	+.84 (21)	1.00									
X_{11}	+.24 (22)	−.25 (0)	−.21 (1)	−.23 (1)	−.01 (13)	−.13 (3)	−.11 (5)	−.18 (2)	−.04 (11)	−.09 (11)	1.00								
X_{12}	−.60 (0)	+.96 (22)	+.63 (22)	+.36 (22)	−.01 (13)	−.01 (8)	+.74 (21)	+.74 (22)	+.01 (10)	+.01 (12)	−.31 (0)	1.00							
X_{13}	−.46 (0)	+.61 (22)	+.91 (22)	+.07 (15)	−.05 (7)	+.07 (14)	+.35 (20)	+.59 (22)	.00 (11)	+.00 (12)	−.21 (0)	+.60 (22)	1.00						
X_{14}	−.08 (7)	+.04 (9)	−.11 (6)	+.52 (22)	+.13 (17)	−.01 (9)	−.07 (7)	−.22 (3)	+.10 (13)	+.03 (13)	+.03 (13)	+.01 (11)	−.10 (5)	1.00					
X_{15}	+.20 (20)	−.11 (5)	+.05 (18)	−.70 (0)	−.02 (10)	−.01 (11)	+.07 (16)	+.14 (19)	−.14 (4)	−.06 (6)	+.02 (13)	−.13 (4)	+.02 (14)	−.6? (0)	1.00				
X_{16}	−.56 (0)	+.80 (22)	+.65 (22)	−.05 (10)	+.16 (18)	−.01 (10)	+.29 (20)	+.99 (22)	−.07 (7)	−.03 (11)	−.17 (2)	+.76 (22)	+.58 (22)	−.21 (3?)	+.13 (3)	1.00			
X_{17}	+.18 (19)	−.19 (1)	−.20 (1)	−.16 (4)	−.01 (9)	−.14 (6)	−.07 (4)	−.11 (4)	−.03 (10)	−.03 (10)	+.82 (22)	−.25 (1)	−.20 (0)	.15 (11)	+.00 (15)	−.11 (4)	1.00		
X_{18}	−.22 (2)	+.28 (22)	+.18 (21)	+.27 (20)	−.01 (8)	−.17 (6)	+.11 (17)	+.30 (22)	+.01 (14)	+.12 (14)	−.21 (4)	+.38 (22)	+.18 (21)	−.13 (3?)	+.00 (10)	+.29 (22)	−.05 (7)	1.00	
X_{19}	−.55 (0)	+.91 (22)	+.58 (22)	+.26 (21)	−.01 (11)	+.09 (13)	+.28 (21)	+.69 (22)	.00 (11)	−.00 (12)	−.25 (0)	+.91 (22)	+.56 (22)	+.09 (14)	−.14 (5)	+.69 (22)	−.25 (0)	−.03 (11)	1.00

Note: Numbers in parentheses refer to number of positive relationships between the pairs of variables.

each pair of X variables (X_2 on X_3, X_2 on X_4, and so forth). These simple relationships are summarized in matrix form in Table 16.[11] The figure $-.59$ in the first column is, for example, the weighted average of the twenty-two simple correlations of Y on X_2; $-.47$ is the weighted average of twenty-two simple correlations of Y on X_3, and so forth. Under the column labeled X_2, $+.61$ is the weighted average of the twenty-two simple correlations of X_2 and X_3, and so forth for each and every pair of X variables. The number in parenthesis under each such average correlation is the number of times the relationship between the pair of variables in question was positive. Thus, the correlation between X_2 and X_8 was positive in each and every cross section, whereas the correlation between Y and X_8 was positive in none, i.e., it was consistently negative.

A summary of this matrix follows.

1. Of the eighteen (substantive) variables, the following nine were consistently correlated with yield (See Table 17): X_{12}, X_2, X_{16}, X_{19}, X_8, X_3, X_{13}, X_4, and X_{11}. Of these nine variables, five were "size" variables and two were "duration" variables.

2. Five variables were slightly but nevertheless more or less consistently correlated with yield: X_{18}, X_5, X_{15}, X_{17}, and X_7.

3. Four variables appeared not to be correlated at all with yield: X_{14}, X_6, X_9, and X_{10}.

In addition, the matrix indicates that, as one would expect, substantial intercorrelations existed among the "independent" variables and especially within certain broad classes of variables. Tables 18 and 19 summarize these "grouped" intercorrelations.

1. The *size* variables (X_2, X_8, X_{12}, X_{16}, X_{19}) were all highly intercorrelated and all were highly correlated with yield.

2. The *duration* variables (X_3, X_{13}) were highly intercorrelated and both were highly correlated with yield. In addition, *both* duration variables were highly correlated with *all* the size variables.

3. The *financial security variables* really fall into two subgroups: X_4, X_{14}, X_{15} on the one hand, and X_{11} and X_{17} on the other. The two subgroups are only slightly intercorrelated.

[11] Quarter of year (X_1) is not included in Table 16.

TABLE 17

*Industrial: Weighted Average, Correlation of Yield with Each
Independent Variable, and Number of Plus Signs, 1951–61*

	Variables[a]	Correlation with Yield	Number of Plus Signs
X_{12}	EBIT	-.60	0
X_2	Total capitalization	-.59	0
X_{16}	Average size	-.56	0
X_{19}	Sales	-.55	0
X_8	Size of issue	-.54	0
X_3	Average term	-.47	0
X_{13}	Maturity	-.46	0
X_4	Times pro-forma interest earned	-.33	1
X_{11}	Coefficient of variation: ratio EBIT to sales	+.24	22
X_{18}	Ratio EBIT to sales	-.22	2
X_5	Type of security	-.22	4
X_{15}	Ratio pro-forma long-term debt to pro-forma total capitalization	+.20	20
X_{17}	Coefficient of variation: EBIT	+.18	19
X_7	Years nonrefundable	-.14	4
X_{14}	Ratio of working capital to pro-forma long-term debt	-.08 -.08	7
X_6	Industrial classification	-.07	7
X_9	Relative trend: EBIT	-.07	5
X_{10}	Relative trend: ratio of EBIT to sales	-.04	9

[a] Quarter of year (X_1) not included.

TABLE 18

Industrials: Weighted Average Correlations Among Various Size and Duration Variables, 1951–61

| | Y | Size Variables | | | | | Duration Variables | |
		X_2	X_8	X_{12}	X_{16}	X_{19}	X_3	X_{13}
X	1.00							
X_2	−.59 (0)	1.00						
X_8	−.54 (0)	+.81 (22)	1.00					
X_{12}	−.60 (0)	+.96 (22)	+.74 (22)	1.00				
X_{16}	−.56 (0)	+.80 (22)	+.99 (22)	+.76 (22)	1.00			
X_{19}	−.55 (0)	+.91 (22)	+.69 (22)	+.91 (22)	+.69 (22)	1.00		
X_3	−.47 (0)	+.61 (22)	+.63 (22)	+.63 (22)	+.65 (22)	+.58 (22)	1.00	
X_{13}	−.46 (0)	+.61 (22)	+.59 (22)	+.60 (22)	+.58 (22)	+.56 (22)	+.91 (22)	1.00

4. The *profitability* variables (X_{11}, X_{12}, X_{18}) were not markedly intercorrelated.

5. The two *growth* variables (X_9 and X_{10}) were moderately intercorrelated.

THE STEPWISE REGRESSIONS

To this point, three things have been done: (1) a hypothesis has been formulated and tested and found reasonably satisfactory; (2) the cross-section periods have been chosen so as to "optimize" number of cross sections and degrees of freedom; (3) simple correlations have been obtained and averaged over the twenty-two cross sections, the dependent variable on each "independent"

TABLE 19

*Industrials: Weighted Average Correlations Within
Various Classes of Independent Variables*

	Financial Security					Variability		
	Y	X_4	X_{14}	X_{15}		Y	X_{11}	X_{17}
Y	1.00				Y	1.00		
X_4	−.33 (1)	1.00			X_{11}	+.24 (22)	1.00	
X_{14}	−.08 (7)	+.52 (22)	1.00		X_{17}	+.18 (19)	+.82 (22)	1.00
X_{15}	+.20 (20)	−.70 (0)	−.67 (0)	1.00				

	Profitability					Growth		
	Y	X_{12}	X_{18}			Y	X_9	X_{10}
Y	1.00				Y	1.00		
X_{12}	−.60 (0)	1.00			X_9	−.07 (5)	1.00	
X_{18}	−.22 (2)	+.38 (22)	1.00		X_{10}	−.04 (9)	+.84 (22)	1.00

variable and each independent variable on each of the other independent variables.

These simple correlations have identified those independent variables which are most likely to be important in explaining variations in yield. They have also suggested rather strongly that some of the "independent" variables are highly intercorrelated and that, therefore, not all the variables which seem important may really be so when the others are held constant.

The next step in the procedure responds, therefore, to the following question: Which variables are and which are not really necessary to a satisfactory explanation of variation in yield, time held constant? This question, in turn, has two parts. First, of those variables that are intercorrelated, which are the most important and, of the

rest, which in fact contribute something *additional* to our understanding of variation in yield? For example, X_2 and X_{12} are both
highly correlated with yield but both are "size" variables and they
are highly correlated with each other. Are both necessary? And
what about the other size variables? Do they make any contribution to an explanation of variation in yield after the separate effects
of X_2 and X_{12} have been taken into account?

Second, what about the variables which seem to be acting independently (e.g., X_7), or which are correlated little, if at all, with
the other independent variables? Are they really making a *separate*
contribution to our understanding of variation in yield?

In an attempt to answer these questions, the variables were introduced successively, in each cross section, in the order of their
subscripts as given in Table 17. For the purpose of deciding which
variable should be introduced first, guidance was provided by the
simple correlation matrix. In effect, the first substantive variable
introduced was a size variable (X_2); the second, a duration variable
(X_3); the third, a financial security variable (X_4), and so forth.
The second size variable (X_{12}) was not introduced until at least one
variable from each other group had been introduced.

Thus, for the first cross section (i.e., the first half of 1951), Y
was regressed on X_1 and a regression coefficient for X_1 obtained;
Y was then regressed on X_1 and X_2 together, coefficients for both
X_1 and X_2 being obtained; X_3 was then introduced, and so on
through X_{19}. Therefore, for the first half of 1951, nineteen regression equations were obtained—the first with one variable, the
second with two, etc. One set of nineteen such equations was thus
obtained for each of the twenty-two half years in 1951–61.

Table 20 gives R^2, F, Probability of F, and degrees of freedom
for *the nineteenth equation* in each of these twenty-two cross sections.[12]

---

[12] Comparison of the R^2's in Table 20 with those given in Table 15 indicate
some deterioration, especially in 1956. In general, it seems clear that the basic
hypothesis tends to explain less variation in yield when the length of the cross
section, in terms of time, is increased. This, of course, is what one would expect,

TABLE 20

Industrials: Twenty-Two Regressions, Yield on Nineteen Variables, R^2, F, Probability of F, Degrees of Freedom, Semiannually, 1951–61

	R^2	F	$P_F \lessgtr$	Degrees of Freedom
1951				
1	.783	12.2	.01	64
2	.876	11.4	.01	31
1952				
1	.769	9.8	.01	56
2	.815	6.2	.01	27
1953				
1	.709	4.7	.01	37
2	.797	5.6	.01	27
1954				
1	.743	8.7	.01	57
2	.805	8.7	.01	40
1955				
1	.707	5.3	.01	42
2	.766	9.3	.01	54
1956				
1	.560	2.7	.01	40
2	.590	4.9	.01	64
1957				
1	.484	1.8	.05	36
2	.843	2.0	.10	7
1958				
1	.691	3.4	.01	29
2	.714	4.3	.01	33
1959				
1	.736	2.5	.05	17
2	.799	4.8	.01	23
1960				
1	.534	1.3		21
2	.663	4.0	.01	39
1961				
1	.721	7.3	.01	54
2	.697	2.9	.05	24

The principal product of these twenty-two stepwise regressions was a succession of "t" statistics as follows: the initial "t" obtained for any given variable was the "t" which resulted when that variable was entered into the regression—i.e., when X_2 was entered into the regression in the first cross section, a "t" was obtained which constituted a test of the significance of X_2 given X_1. One such initial "t" for X_2 was obtained for *each of the twenty-two cross sections,* or, in other words, a total of twenty-two "t's" bearing on the significance of X_2 and X_1. The same procedure was followed for each variable X_3 through X_{19}. Table 21 gives these *initial* "t's" for each variable and each cross section.

Using the initial "t's," three tests were then run: a $\bar{t}$ test, a sign test, and what might be called a "distribution of t's" test.

1. The $\bar{t}$ test, was designed to ascertain whether some given variable, X_1, added *consistently and significantly* (in the statistical sense) to regression when entered into the regression, i.e., given the preceding variables. For example, if b_1 (the coefficient of variable X_1) showed a $\bar{t}$ greater than 2.00, this would mean that a large proportion of the twenty-two signs were in one direction *and* that a large proportion of the individual t's were high. Inasmuch as each individual t is a test of *statistical* significance, a high $\bar{t}$ constitutes strong evidence that the variable in question was consistently (i.e., over the twenty-two cross sections) statistically significant when entered. Table 21 shows, for example, that, when entered, X_2 produced twenty-one t's equal to or less than -2.00 and a $\bar{t}$ of -5.42; when X_3 was entered, it produced six t's equal to or less than -2.00 and a $\bar{t}$ of -1.01.[13]

2. Variables which show a low $\bar{t}$ may, however, be significant. A low $\bar{t}$ means merely that such variables are not *statistically* significant, i.e., that the amount of variation being explained by

given the fact that the longer the cross section, the greater the expected variation in yield with respect to time. But see below, Table 24.

[13] Strictly, probabilities rather than "t's" should have been distributed and averaged, using Fisher's technique, in order to give due weight to differing degrees of freedom. This refinement did not seem worth the large amount of additional computation which it would have required. See last column of Table 20.

TABLE 21

Industrials: Significance of Each Variable, $X_2 - X_{19}$, When that Variable Was Introduced into Regression, Semiannually, 1951–61[a]

	t_{X_2}	t_{X_3}	t_{X_4}	t_{X_5}	t_{X_6}	t_{X_7}	t_{X_8}	t_{X_9}	$t_{X_{10}}$
1951									
1	-9.90	-2.19	-3.27	-4.25	-3.12	+ .92	-1.99	-1.74	+1.02
2	-9.54	+1.30	-4.38	-1.55	-1.22	-2.13	+1.30	- .57	+ .48
1952									
1	-6.81	+ .60	-5.00	-4.56	-1.05	+1.85	-2.30	+ .93	+2.35
2	-6.38	+ .19	- .12	-4.53	- .54	- .30	- .12	- .16	- .10
1953									
1	-6.09	-1.25	- .52	-3.00	-3.36	+1.63	+ .72	- .98	- .32
2	-3.75	-3.32	-3.97	-3.51	-1.61	+1.80	-1.89	- .002	+ .99
1954									
1	-6.20	-2.01	-1.83	-2.02	-1.04	+3.26	-2.77	+ .37	+1.02
2	-5.60	- .89	-2.61	-4.54	-2.92	+2.76	-3.30	+ .14	- .02
1955									
1	-7.62	-1.22	-3.38	-1.06	- .84	+1.68	- .65	- .12	+ .64
2	-6.92	-1.62	-4.22	-5.74	-1.43	- .13	- .28	- .81	-2.59
1956									
1	-2.18	-2.60	-1.53	+1.13	+2.31	+ .38	-2.42	-2.65	-1.06
2	-6.46	-1.09	-2.63	-0.06	-1.21	-2.03	-1.75	- .49	+ .47
1957									
1	-1.88	+ .20	-2.93	-2.99	-1.34	+ .43	-1.53	+ .52	+ .37
2	-2.69	+0.15	- .69	-2.11	- .85	- .66	-1.23	+ .26	+ .21
1958									
1	-2.94	-2.23	-2.76	- .89	- .13	+1.15	-2.44	+ .34	- .37
2	-6.00	-1.05	-1.80	-1.73	+ .57	+2.21	+ .54	+ .28	-1.11
1959									
1	-3.51	-1.29	-0.06	+ .47	-1.61	+1.65	- .48	-1.72	+1.04
2	-4.11	-1.83	-3.44	-2.41	- .31	- .39	-2.00	- .42	- .32
1960									
1	-2.52	+ .29	-2.08	- .74	-1.19	+ .20	-1.18	-1.30	+0.92
2	-7.00	-1.04	-1.08	-1.13	- .91	+1.14	+1.53	- .06	+1.01
1961									
1	-5.23	-3.18	-4.95	-1.59	+1.15	+ .04	-1.34	+1.37	+ .12
2	-5.88	+ .49	-1.02	- .64	+ .79	- .71	-1.37	- .38	- .47
$\bar{t}$	-5.42	-1.07	-2.47	-2.09	-0.90	+0.67	-1.14	-0.33	+0.13

(continued)

TABLE 21 (concluded)

	$^{t}X_{11}$	$^{t}X_{12}$	$^{t}X_{13}$	$^{t}X_{14}$	$^{t}X_{15}$	$^{t}X_{16}$	$^{t}X_{17}$	$^{t}X_{18}$	$^{t}X_{19}$
1951									
1	- .19	+ .51	+1.00	- .60	- .37	- .53	- .61	+ .10	+ .18
2	- .86	+2.45	+ .32	- .29	-1.63	- .06	-1.14	+ .08	+1.75
1952									
1	+ .62	+ .68	+ .09	+1.91	-1.11	+ .69	+ .81	-1.04	+ .99
2	-1.76	+2.25	- .55	+1.31	- .26	- .91	-1.65	+ .52	-1.96
1953									
1	- .98	+ .73	-1.55	+1.29	- .25	+ .03	+1.53	- .36	+ .64
2	- .24	+1.05	- .90	- .82	-1.09	+1.46	- .42	- .04	+ .51
1954									
1	-1.35	+1.85	+ .93	-1.43	- .61	-2.03	+2.55	-1.03	-2.60
2	+2.23	+ .46	-1.49	-1.62	- .66	+ .57	+ .52	+ .10	- .21
1955									
1	+ .66	+2.36	- .09	- .35	- .86	- .62	+1.36	+ .34	-1.85
2	+1.07	- .67	- .16	+ .58	+ .74	- .77	- .07	+ .48	+1.04
1956									
1	-1.23	+1.57	+2.04	-1.14	+ .89	- .26	+ .55	+ .25	- .10
2	+ .48	- .04	+ .76	- .22	-1.33	+1.17	+ .33	-1.91	+ .69
1957									
1	- .02	+ .05	+ .32	+1.42	-1.94	+ .40	- .84	- .84	+ .45
2	+1.58	- .20	+1.96	-1.01	+ .28	- .03	+ .44	-2.79	+ .44
1958									
1	+ .96	-3.22	- .53	+ .83	-2.34	- .26	+ .26	- .41	- .79
2	+ .25	- .93	- .48	+ .13	+1.66	+ .47	+1.07	+1.24	+2.52
1959									
1	+ .30	- .72	-1.74	+1.20	- .01	+1.74	-1.86	-1.28	- .42
2	+1.54	- .19	- .60	+2.37	- .02	- .55	+ .86	-1.55	- .14
1960									
1	+ .56	+ .91	- .04	-1.87	+ .53	+ .52	+1.40	+ .01	-1.29
2	- .72	+ .63	-1.57	+ .91	- .25	- .37	+ .67	-1.39	-2.38
1961									
1	+ .85	+1.55	-1.47	+ .97	+ .38	+ .42	-2.17	-2.54	-1.38
2	+1.11	+1.27	-1.79	+ .85	+ .92	- .61	+ .99	+ .86	+ .52
$\bar{t}$	+0.22	+0.56	-0.34	+0.20	-0.33	-0.02	+0.18	-0.51	-0.15

[a]The numbers given in this table are t's $\left(= \dfrac{b_i}{\sigma_{b_i}} \right)$.

such variables is relatively small. In addition, any variable, whether or not it bears any real relation to the dependent variable, will add something to the sum of squares for regression, simply because of sampling error. The second test then, *the sign test,* is aimed at identifying those variables which, although not statistically significant, are consistently adding small amounts to regression. This test is based on the presumption that if a variable is merely a random number (i.e., if it bears no real relation to the dependent variable) its twenty-two initial "t's" should show roughly equal numbers of plus and minus signs. If its "t's" show an unexpectedly large number of plus or minus signs, a presumption would be created that it (the underlying variable) was *not* a random number, but, rather, bore some consistent relation to the dependent variable. Table 22 indicates that b_6 and b_8 (in addition to b_2, b_4, and b_5) showed strong significance by this test, and b_3, b_7, b_{12}, b_{13}, and b_{15}, marginal significance.

3. It is altogether conceivable, however, that some variable which was not important in the early part of the period became so later, or vice versa; or that some variable, X_j, occasionally acts as a proxy for some other variable, X_i, which latter is important most of the time but not always, or less important at some times than at others. If some given variable, not significant by either of the above two tests, showed an unusually large number of very high or very low t values, that variable was also presumed to be significant when entered. X_{12}, for example, showed a low $\bar{t}$ ($+0.56$) and fifteen plus signs but, on the other hand, three t's larger than $+2.00$ (Table 23).

Any variable which failed to show significance by at least one of the above three tests was eliminated from further consideration; it was assumed to be nothing more than a random number. This does not mean, of course, that such variables were, *in fact,* random numbers (although they may have been so); it means merely *that given the preceding variables,* such variables were behaving as *if they were* random numbers. Thus, given X_2, which showed

TABLE 22

Industrials: Number of Plus and Minus Signs Obtained on Partial Regression Coefficients and Binomial Probability of Obtaining at Least Larger Number if Actual Probability Is .50

Coefficient	No. of Plus Signs	No. of Minus Signs	$P_{B \overset{=}{<}}$
b_2	0	22	.000
b_3	7	15	.067
b_4	0	22	.000
b_5	2	20	.000
b_6	4	18	.002
b_7	15	7	.067
b_8	4	18	.002
b_9	8	14	.143
b_{10}	13	9	.262
b_{11}	13	9	.262
b_{12}	15	7	.067
b_{13}	7	15	.067
b_{14}	12	10	.416
b_{15}	7	15	.067
b_{16}	10	12	.416
b_{17}	13	9	.262
b_{18}	10	12	.416
b_{19}	11	11	.584

high significance when entered, X_{19}, also a size variable, consistently added nothing to regression. This does not mean, of course, that had X_{19} been entered *first* it would have added nothing to regression. Given the high degree of correlation between X_2 and X_{19}, the latter would almost surely have shown high significance, had it been entered first.

TABLE 23

*Industrials: $\bar{t}$'s and Distribution of t's When Entered,
Partial Regression Coefficients on X_2-X_{19}*

Coefficient	$\bar{t}$	Per Cent $\stackrel{=}{>} +2.00$	Per Cent $\stackrel{=}{<} -2.00$
b_2	-5.42	$--$	95.5
b_3	-1.01		27.3
b_4	-2.47	$--$	59.1
b_5	-2.09	$--$	50.0
b_6	-0.90	4.5	13.6
b_7	$+0.67$	13.6	9.1
b_8	-1.14	$--$	22.7
b_9	-0.33	$--$	4.5
b_{10}	$+0.13$	4.5	4.5
b_{11}	$+0.22$	4.5	$--$
b_{12}	$+0.56$	13.6	4.5
b_{13}	-0.34	$--$	4.5
b_{14}	$+0.20$	4.5	$--$
b_{15}	-0.33	$--$	4.5
b_{16}	-0.02	$--$	4.5
b_{17}	$+0.18$	4.5	4.5
b_{18}	-0.51	$--$	9.1
b_{19}	-0.15	4.5	9.1

In summary: (1) by the $\bar{t}$ test, three variables showed clear significance—X_2, X_4, and X_5 (Table 21); (2) by the sign test, seven additional variables seemed significant or on the borderline of being so—X_3, X_6, X_7, X_8, X_{12}, X_{13}, and X_{15} (Table 22); (3) by the distribution of t's test, no *additional* variables appeared to be even marginally significant (Table 23).

In order to catch any coefficient which might have failed to show significance by the sign test simply because it was trending from above zero to below zero, or vice versa, weighted trends were fitted to those coefficients which had not otherwise shown significance—b_9, b_{10}, b_{11}, b_{14}, b_{16}, b_{17}, b_{18}, and b_{19}.[14] None showed trend.

Last, each of the coefficients which had shown no significance by the above tests when entered was examined in the light of *subsequent* variables. None showed significance as variables were added.

The next question was: Are all the variables which are presumed to be significant *when entered* really necessary? For example, three size variables, X_2, X_8, and X_{12}, showed significance when entered, but of course X_8 and X_{12} were not in the regression when X_2 was entered and X_{12} was not in the regression when X_8 was entered. Possibly, therefore, X_2 is not necessary given X_8; and X_8, in its turn, may not be necessary given X_{12}. This means that the significance of X_2 must be examined in the light of X_8 and X_{12}, and the significance of X_8, in the light of X_{12}.

RERUNS ON SIGNIFICANT VARIABLES

In response to the above question, the regressions were rerun quarterly on the ten significant variables plus month of quarter. Month of quarter was included as a variable in order to hold time constant to some extent within each quarter.[15] Given the fact that both the ratio of EBIT to total interest (X_4) and EBIT itself (X_{12}) showed significance when entered, X_4 was redefined so as to avoid including the same variable twice and thus dividing its effect between two coefficients. The redefined variable X_{4r} became simply total pro-forma interest.

The results of these forty-four regressions are given in Tables 24 and 25. On the whole, the results given in Table 24 are satisfactory and represent some improvement over those of the twenty-two

---

[14] Each coefficient was weighted inversely as to its variance.
[15] All variables were introduced simultaneously and *not* stepwise.

TABLE 24

Industrials: Forty-Four Regressions, Yield on Eleven
Variables, R^2, F, Probability of F, Degrees of Freedom,
Quarterly, 1951–61

Year and Quarter	R^2	F	$P_F \lessgtr$	Degree of Freedom
1951				
1	.801	11.3	.01	31
2	.785	9.6	.01	29
3	.951	22.6	.01	13
4	.910	15.6	.01	17
1952				
1	.766	8.9	.01	30
2	.806	9.1	.01	24
3	.869	9.0	.01	15
4	.872	5.6	.01	9
1953				
1	.759	4.0	.01	14
2	.814	8.0	.01	20
3	.904	6.0	.05	7
4	.759	4.6	.01	16
1954				
1	.677	4.6	.01	24
2	.704	6.5	.01	30
3	.870	8.5	.01	14
4	.792	8.3	.01	24
1955				
1	.766	4.7	.01	16
2	.755	6.4	.01	23
3	.889	16.1	.01	22
4	.643	4.9	.01	30
1956				
1	.671	2.2	a	12
2	.643	3.9	.01	24
3	.594	4.8	.01	36
4	.626	3.8	.01	25

(continued)

TABLE 24 (concluded)

Year and Quarter	R^2	F	$P_{F\lessgtr}^=$	Degree of Freedom
1957				
1	.542	1.8	a	17
2	.588	1.9	a	15
3	.986	6.7	.01	1
4	.796	1.1	a	3
1958				
1	.893	6.1	.01	8
2	.757	5.1	.01	18
3	.789	6.1	.01	18
4	.884	7.6	.01	11
1959				
1	.774	0.9	a	3
2	.566	1.4	a	12
3	.895	9.3	.01	12
4	.778	2.9	a	9
1960				
1	.856	1.1	a	2
2	.424	1.1	a	16
3	.704	2.6	.05	12
4	.701	4.9	.01	23
1961				
1	.803	8.9	.01	24
2	.540	2.9	.05	27
3	.654	2.4	a	14
4	.723	1.4	a	6

[a]P_F is greater than .05.

semiannual regressions (Table 20). In sixteen of forty-four regressions (or about 36 per cent), R^2 was greater than .80, whereas this was true in only four cross sections when the regressions were run semiannually. In addition, thirty-two R^2's (or about 73 per cent) were greater than .70 when the regressions were run quarterly

TABLE 25

*Industrials: Forty-Four Regressions, Yield on Eleven
Variables, Number of Times t Was Greater Than +2.00 or
Less Than −2.00 and Distribution of Plus and Minus Signs
of Coefficients*

| Coefficient | t Greater Than +2.00 | t Less Than −2.00 | Distribution of Signs | | $P_B \lessgtr^a$ |
			Plus	Minus	
b_2	1	8	11	33	.001
b_3	1	6	14	30	.02
$b_{4r}{}^b$	12	0	34	10	.001
b_5	0	11	8	36	.0001
b_6	0	5	14	30	.02
b_7	2	2	28	16	.05
b_8	1	11	14	30	.02
b_{12}	1	4	8	36	.0001
b_{13}	1	1	20	24	.33
b_{15}	0	4	18	26	.15

[a]Probability of obtaining at least larger number of signs (either plus or minus) if true probability equals .50.

[b]Small r indicates redefined version of variable used. See text.

as compared with fifteen (or about 68 per cent) when the regressions were run semiannually. In brief, narrowing the cross section from six to three months has, on the whole, reduced the error, despite the fact that the number of variables has been substantially reduced.

Table 25 summarizes various data bearing on the significance of the variables included in these "reruns." The first two columns indicate the number of times t was greater than +2.00 or less than −2.00. The coefficient on X_2, for example, was greater than +2.00

in one cross section and less than -2.00 in eight cross sections, the coefficient on X_3 was greater than $+2.00$ in one cross section and less than -2.00 in six cross sections, and so forth for each other variable. The next two columns tabulate the number of plus and minus signs of each coefficient over the forty-four cross-sections, and the last column gives the probability of obtaining the larger number of signs. Thus, of the forty-four coefficients on X_2, thirty-three were negative and eleven positive. The probability of obtaining the thirty-three minus signs, if the true probability is .50, is .001 and so forth for each other variable. Each of the ten variables, except X_{13}, shows significance by either the t's test or the sign test. X_{13} showed trend at $P < .02$.

Importance of Variables

The foregoing analysis has accomplished two things: (1) it has separated the "significant" from the "nonsignificant" variables and (2) it has provided us with a series of forty-four quarterly predictive equations, which will be used below to compute series on yields on direct placements. It has told us nothing, however, about the *importance* of each variable, that is, which variables are capable of having a substantial impact on yield and which are not. Thus, if a coefficient is small and the variability of the associated variable is also small, the impact on yield will not be great, even if the coefficient is highly significant statistically.

To assess the importance of each variable in this sense, three steps were taken. First, an over-all regression was run for the period as a whole on all the significant variables, with X_4 redefined as indicated above. In this regression, time was held approximately constant by using the monthly yield on Aaa corporates (Moody's) as a variable.[16] The results of this over-all regression are given in

---

[16] We might alternatively have averaged each b_i over its forty-four sample values, weighting each sample value inversely as to its variance, or have used that value of each b_i which, of the forty-four sample values, showed the strongest significance. AAA corporates were used because they seemed to conform, better than other available series, to the movements of direct placements.

TABLE 26

Industrials: "Over-All" Regression, Log Y on Eleven
Variables, Regression Coefficients, Standard Errors, and
Tests of Significance

Coefficient	$\bar{b}$	$\sigma_{\bar{b}}$	t	$P_t{}^a \lesseqqgtr$
Intercept	+1.1816	.0361	+32.70	.001
b_1	+ .7995	.0146	+54.85	.001
b_2	- .0475	.0081	- 5.84	.001
b_3	- .0228	.0143	- 1.59	.15
b_{4r}	+ .0683	.0071	+ 9.58	.001
b_5	- .0232	.0028	- 8.32	.001
b_6	- .0178	.0046	- 3.91	.001
b_7	+ .0010	.0003	+ 3.59	.001
b_8	- .0195	.0029	- 6.76	.001
b_{12}	- .0322	.0047	- 6.87	.001
b_{13}	- .0212	.0155	- 1.37	.20
b_{15}	- .0349	.0077	- 4.54	.001

[a]With 1,271 degrees of freedom, two tailed.
For this regression, R^2 = .806, F = 481.1, and P_F = <.001.

Table 26.[17] Second, each of the regression coefficients given by the over-all regression was multiplied by the standard deviation of the appropriate X_i. Finally, the antilog of each product was obtained (without regard to the sign of that product). The results are given in Table 27.

Column 1 of Table 27 lists the various $\bar{b}_i$'s; column 2, the σ of each X_i; and column 3 the product of each $\bar{b}$ multiplied by the

[17] Two variables which were deemed significant in the cross sections, showed only slight significance over-all—X_3 and X_{13}. The coefficients on these variables fluctuated around zero (see Chart D-1). The cross-section analysis does not, of course, hold expectations as to the future course of interest rates constant and perhaps the signs of these two coefficients were sensitive to such expectations. See Appendix A.

TABLE 27

Industrials: Percentage Impact of Each Variable on Yield
When that Variable Increased by One Standard Deviation

Variable	b_i (1)	σ_{x_i} (2)	$b_i \sigma_{x_i}$ (3)	Antilog of Col. 3[a] (4)
X_2	-.0475	1.7523	-.08323	1.09
X_3	-.0228	.3855	-.00879	1.01
X_{4r}	+.0683	1.7018	+.11623	1.12
X_5	-.0232	.8237	-.01911	1.02
X_6	-.0178	.4857	-.00865	1.01
X_7	+.0010	8.5396	+.00854	1.01
X_8	-.0195	1.4262	-.02781	1.03
X_{12}	-.0322	1.7823	-.05739	1.06
X_{13}	-.0212	.3369	-.00714	1.01
X_{15}	-.0349	.5410	-.01888	1.02

[a]Signs ignored.

corresponding σ of each X. Column 4 gives the antilog of this product and represents the approximate percentage change in yield which would be produced by an increase in X_i of an amount equal to one standard deviation.

The ten variables, ranked in the order of their respective percentage impact on yield, are X_{4r}, X_2, X_{12}, X_8, X_5, X_{15}, X_3, X_6, X_7, and X_{13}.

The Yield Series

With the foregoing results in hand, two sets of series were constructed: a set of *cross-classified* series and a set of *computed* series. The cross-classified series hold (approximately) constant just two significant variables—albeit two of the most important—

CHART 6

Industrials: System of Cross Classification Used to Construct
Seven Cross-Classified Yield Series, 1951–61

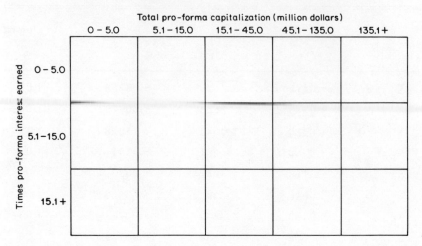

whereas the computed series hold rigidly constant all ten significant variables. The cross-classified series are relatively easy to understand and construct and provide "reasonable homogeneity" through time.[18]

THE CROSS-CLASSIFIED SERIES

The procedure used to construct the cross-classified series involved four main steps.

First, the X_4 variable was put back into its original form—as a measure of coverage. Doing so made it possible to take account of three rather than just two of the most important variables.

Quarterly regressions were then run on X_4, as so defined, and on X_2 alone. Weighted averages struck over the set of forty-four coefficients for each variable were, respectively, $-.0288$ and $-.0231$.[19]

---

[18] On the average over the forty-four quarters, X_2 and X_4 together explain about 45 per cent of variation in yield. The ten significant variables explain about 75 per cent.

[19] Both coefficients showed trend over the period but the relationship between

Second, class intervals were established over X_2 and X_4, based on the foregoing weighted average regression coefficients. These class intervals are given in Chart 6. The fact that the regression coefficients on X_2 and X_4 were close to being equal meant that the effect on yield of a given percentage *increase* in (e.g.) X_2 would be almost precisely offset by a corresponding percentage *decrease* in X_4 and this, in turn, meant that the cells lying along any given left-to-right diagonal (see Chart 6) could be regarded, other things being equal, as representing roughly equivalent "quality." Thus, all the issues falling in each of the cells lying along diagonal number 4 were presumed to represent equivalent "quality" in this sense—and correspondingly with each of the other four left-to-right diagonals. This is equivalent to saying that the sum of the logarithms (i.e., log X_2 + log X_4), taken at the means of the two classes, is approximately equal from one cell to another along any left-to-right diagonal. The *size* of each class interval was chosen so as to allow a "spread," measured at the mean of each interval, of about 5 per cent in yield between diagonals.[20]

Third, the observations were deposited each into their appropriate cells. Simple arithmetic averages were then struck along each diagonal for each quarter. This procedure produced seven quarterly yield series.

These series, however, showed a fairly large number of inconsistencies, roughly half of which were due to the small number of observations in some series in some quarters. Finally, therefore, the seven classes were consolidated into three, so as to provide a strong "middle" series containing about 50 per cent of the observations and "lower" and "upper" series each containing roughly 25 per cent of the observations. The three resulting series are set forth

them was, for all practical purposes, stable. The ratio of b_2 to b_4 was 1.25 in the first quarter of 1951 and 1.20 in the last quarter of 1961.

[20] In addition, some 200 observations, which were not included in the original regressions, were added at this point. These observations were not included originally because in each case some data were missing. After the regressions were run, however, these 200 observations were found to be complete in the necessary respects.

TABLE 28

Industrials: *Yields on Direct Placements, Cross Classified,*
by Class, Quarterly, 1951–61

Year and Quarter	Class I (1)	Class II (2)	Class III (3)	Composite[a] (4)
1951				
1	3.21	3.78	4.11	3.70
2	3.18	3.93	4.63	4.01
3	3.55	3.99	4.84	4.13
4	3.70	4.16	4.75	4.20
1952				
1	3.88	4.33	4.73	4.31
2	3.78	4.27	4.75	4.27
3	3.72	4.31	4.86	4.30
4	3.88	4.20	5.06	4.38
1953				
1	3.94	4.59	4.77	4.43
2	4.29	4.53	4.86	4.56
3	4.48	4.67	5.37	4.84
4	4.45	4.57	5.10	4.71
1954				
1	4.03	4.57	5.02	4.54
2	4.01	4.26	4.57	4.28
3	3.72	4.07	4.68	4.16
4	3.73	4.25	4.34	4.11
1955				
1	3.73	4.17	4.79	4.23
2	3.83	4.23	5.16	4.41
3	3.87	4.24	5.17	4.43
4	4.27	4.55	4.83	4.55
1956				
1	4.46	4.49	4.78	4.58
2	4.48	4.64	4.85	4.66
3	4.30	4.91	5.32	4.84
4	4.81	5.20	5.63	5.21

(continued)

TABLE 28 (concluded)

Year and Quarter	Class I (1)	Class II (2)	Class III (3)	Composite[a] (4)
1957				
1	5.16	5.45	5.54	5.38
2	5.27	5.32	5.75	5.45
3	5.58	5.61	5.98	5.72
4	5.38	5.78	5.83	5.66
1958				
1	5.24	5.42	5.67	5.44
2	4.92	5.50	5.57	5.33
3	4.95	5.37	5.40	5.24
4	5.16	5.67	5.90	5.58
1959				
1	5.20	5.80	6.00	5.67
2	5.50	5.75	5.93	5.73
3	5.65	5.80	6.07	5.84
4	5.98	6.02	6.34	6.11
1960				
1	5.89	6.17	6.38	6.15
2	5.72	6.20	6.11[b]	6.01
3	5.76	6.07	6.39	6.07
4	5.36	5.94	6.13	5.81
1961				
1	5.43	5.92	6.27	5.87
2	5.40	5.59	5.94	5.64
3	5.53	5.70	6.13	5.79
4	5.41	5.62	5.92	5.65

[a]This series is equal to the sum of Classes I, II, and III divided by 3 (the arithmetic mean).

[b]Inconsistency.

CHART 7

Industrials: Yields on Direct Placements, Cross Classified,
by Class, Quarterly, 1951–61

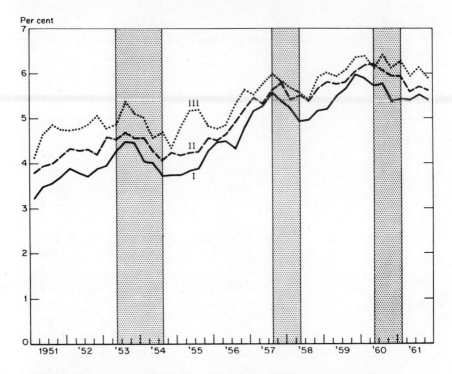

Shaded areas represent business contractions; white areas, expansions.
SOURCE: Table 28.

in Table 28 and Chart 7. Grade I is made up of classes 1, 2, and
3; Grade II, of classes 4 and 5, and Grade III of classes 6 and 7.[21]

[21] A variety of alternative procedures was available for the purpose of reducing
the number of series from seven to three. The means of adjacent *diagonals* could
have been averaged. This procedure would, of course, have given equal weight
to each diagonal. The mean in each *cell*, along each of the three diagonals,
could have been calculated and these means in turn averaged. This procedure
seemed better than the first because it would have given less weight to an
extreme fluctuation along any diagonal. The mean for any given quarter could
simply have been struck, over all the *observations* lying along the diagonals
to be consolidated. This procedure would have given equal weight to *each
observation* and would have further reduced the likelihood that the result in

CHART 8

Industrials: Yields on Direct Placements, Composite Cross Classified, Compared with Yields on FHA Mortgages and Yields on Long-Term Governments, Quarterly, 1951–61

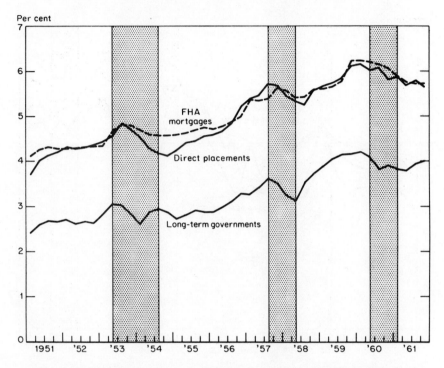

Shaded areas represent business contractions; white areas, expansions.
SOURCE: Table 28; *Federal Reserve Bulletin; Treasury Bulletin.*

A "composite" series, which is simply an arithmetic average, quarterly, of the three series set forth in Table 28, is given in the last column of that table. Charts 8 and 9 compare the movements of this "composite" series with the movements of yields on FHA

any given quarter in any given class would be affected unduly by an extreme observation.

All three procedures were tried. The first produced three inconsistencies and the others, two each. The series did not differ greatly one from another and the one represented by the third procedure, above, was used.

CHART 9

*Industrials: Yields on Direct Placements, Composite Cross
Classified, Compared with Moody's Yields on New Issues
Grades A and Baa, Quarterly, 1951–61*

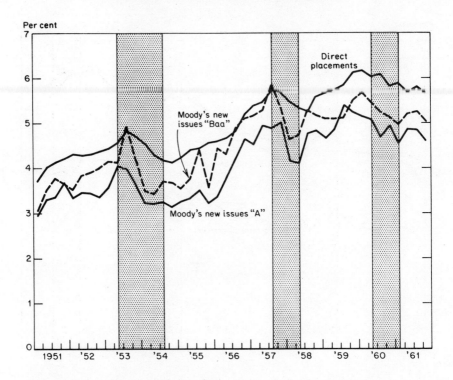

Shaded areas represent business contractions; white areas, expansions.
SOURCE: Table 28 and Moody's Bond Survey.

mortgages, long-term governments, and Moody's new issues "A"
and "Baa."

THE COMPUTED SERIES

Next, values were established, closely approximating the mean
values of the three cross-classified series (see Table 29).[22] These

[22] Of course, any set of arbitrary values might have been used for this
purpose—and any reader who wishes to experiment may do so, subject to the
caveat that the coefficients should not be used outside the range of observations
from which they were derived. The mean values of the cross-classified series

TABLE 29

Industrials: Mean Values Used to Obtain Computed Series, by Class

Variable	Unit	Series Ic	IIc	IIIc
X_2	Million dollars	150.0	20.0	4.0
X_3	Years	10.0	8.0	7.0
X_{4r}	Million dollars	1.2	0.3	0.1
X_5	a	1.5	1.5	1.3
X_6	b	0.6	0.6	0.7
X_7	Years	4.0	5.0	3.0
X_8	Million dollars	16.0	4.0	1.3
X_{12}	Million dollars	20.0	4.0	0.9
X_{13}	Years	18.0	15.0	13.0
X_{15}	Dollars of long-term debt per dollar of total capital	0.31	0.31	0.28

[a]For this variable, first mortgage bonds = 0; second mortgage bonds or debts secured by securities or lease = 1; senior debentures = 2; and subordinated debentures = 3. The figures here are an average of these code numbers.

[b]For industrial classification, durables = 0 and nondurables = 1. The figures here are an average of these code numbers.

values were held rigidly constant for each of the three series through the period. Quarterly yields for each series were then computed, using the forty-four regression equations given by the rerun on the ten significant variables.[23] These computed yields are given in the first three columns of Table 30, and in Chart 10.

were used because (a) comparisons with the cross-classified series might be enlightening and (b) the cross-classified series were equally spaced in terms of "quality" and using their mean values suggested that the computed series would be approximately equally spaced also.

1951–61 values were used for the *individual* series instead of 1956 values (as, below, for the *composite* series) because the 1956 values for the individual series did not appear to be representative.

[23] The series were centered in the middle of the second month of each quarter.

TABLE 30

Industrials: Yields on Direct Placements, Computed,
by Class, Quarterly, 1951–61

Year and Quarter	Class Ic (1)	Class IIc (2)	Class IIIc (3)	Composite[a] (4)
1951				
1	3.27	3.81	4.33	3.80
2	3.26	3.73	4.21	3.73
3	4.17	4.36	5.05	4.53
4	3.29	4.24	5.20	4.24
1952				
1	3.49	4.41	5.34	4.41
2	3.82	4.54	5.26	4.54
3	3.66	4.94	6.27	4.96
4	3.47	4.04	4.57	4.03
1953				
1	3.96	4.50	4.93	4.46
2	4.02	4.84	5.65	4.84
3	4.30	4.55	4.76	4.54
4	4.12	4.65	5.14	4.64
1954				
1	4.26	4.57	4.77	4.53
2	3.56	4.19	4.76	4.17
3	3.70	4.23	4.77	4.23
4	3.55	3.98	4.42	3.98
1955				
1	3.37	4.09	5.10	4.19
2	3.52	3.96	4.37	3.95
3	3.58	4.14	4.72	4.15
4	4.08	4.68	5.29	4.68
1956				
1	4.33	4.46	4.60	4.46
2	4.53	4.57	4.49[b]	4.53
3	4.61	4.77	5.05	4.81
4	4.68	5.33	5.83	5.28

(continued)

TABLE 30 (concluded)

Year and Quarter	Class Ic (1)	Class IIc (2)	Class IIIc (3)	Composite[a] (4)
1957				
1	4.85	5.59	6.30	5.58
2	4.90	5.28	5.64	5.27
3	4.87	6.26	7.94	6.36
4	5.43	6.03	6.40	5.95
1958				
1	5.03	5.48	5.84	5.45
2	4.59	5.31	6.00	5.30
3	4.89	5.50	6.07	5.49
4	5.17	5.47	5.77	5.47
1959				
1	5.03	5.65	6.48	5.72
2	5.38	5.51	5.62	5.50
3	5.44*	5.34	5.36	5.38
4	5.06	5.77	6.32	5.72
1960				
1	4.80	6.11	7.64	6.18
2	4.95	5.28	5.67	5.30
3	4.53	5.73	5.99	5.42
4	5.62	6.17	6.56	6.12
1961				
1	4.99	5.66	6.32	5.66
2	5.23	5.48	5.77	5.49
3	5.19	5.69	6.21	5.70
4	5.33	5.47	5.71	5.50

[a]This series is equal, for each quarter, the sum of Classes Ic, IIc, and IIIc, divided by 3 (arithmetic mean).

[b]Inconsistency.

CHART 10

Industrials: Yields on Direct Placements, Computed, by
Class, Quarterly, 1951–61

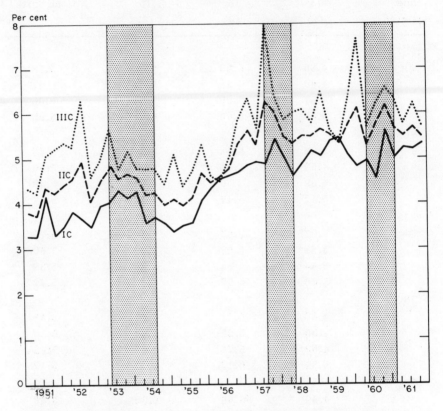

Shaded areas represent business contractions; white areas, expansions.
SOURCE: Table 30.

Chart 11 compares each of the three computed series with its corresponding cross-classified series. On the whole, the general movements of both class I series, except for 1960, and the general movements of both class II series, except for the second and third quarters of 1960, are much the same—although, of course, they need not have been, simply because the cross-classified series do not hold everything constant. There are sharp differences, however, between the two class III series—especially in the first three quarters

CHART 11

*Industrials: Cross-Classified Yield Series Compared with
Computed Yield Series, by Class, Quarterly, 1951–61*

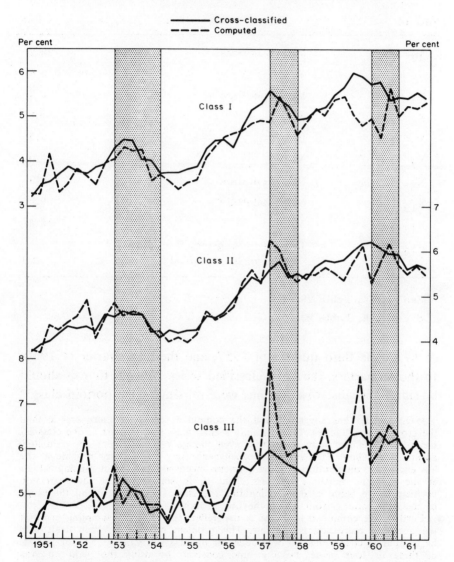

Shaded areas represent business contractions; white areas, expansions.
SOURCE: Tables 28 and 30.

TABLE 31

Industrials: Mean Values Used to Obtain Computed Composite Series

Variable	Unit	Value
X_2	Million dollars	23.2
X_3	Years	9.8
X_{4r}	Million dollars	0.3
X_5	a	1.5
X_6	b	0.6
X_7	Years	6.0
X_8	Million dollars	2.9
X_{12}	Million dollars	2.8
X_{13}	Years	15.3
X_{15}	Dollars of long-term debt per dollar of total capital	.29

[a]See note a, Table 29.
[b]See note b, Table 29.

of 1952, the third quarter of 1957, and the first quarter of 1960. In these quarters, the cross-classified series is lower than it should be simply because observations were missing in the bottom class.[24]

[24] One reader has suggested that the computed series are more erratic than the cross-classified series. This certainly seems to be true at least of the class III series, and this fact may mean that even though residuals were approximately normally distributed, the regression coefficients may not be very reliable at the low end of the distribution in some quarters—primarily because of missing actuals at the low end in those quarters. That is, in some quarters the regression coefficients are being used, in computing the class III series, beyond the range of the observations from which they were derived.

Further, the computed series of course reflect the effect of sampling error in the quarterly regression coefficients. This problem might have been dealt with by computing coefficients (as was done for financials in Chapter 5), for periods of three or four years, holding time constant, by using the yield on Aaa corporates (or a similar series) as a variable, Unhappily, additional runs along these lines were beyond the resources of the present study. They might well be worthwhile, however, as part of any attempt to bring and keep the present series up to date.

TABLE 32

Industrials: Three Composite Yield Series Compared with Each Other and with Average Actual Yields in Sample, Quarterly, 1951–61

Year and Quarter	C_1 (1)	C_2 (2)	C_3 (3)	C_4 (4)
1951				
1	3.70	3.80	3.73	3.69
2	4.01	3.73	3.25	3.83
3	4.13	4.53	4.32	4.28
4	4.20	4.24	3.93	4.05
1952				
1	4.31	4.41	4.17	4.21
2	4.27	4.54	4.36	4.10
3	4.30	4.96	4.27	4.34
4	4.38	4.03	4.00	4.20
1953				
1	4.43	4.46	4.35	4.46
2	4.56	4.84	4.53	4.54
3	4.84	4.54	4.40	4.76
4	4.71	4.64	4.58	4.58
1954				
1	4.54	4.53	4.38	4.47
2	4.28	4.17	4.21	4.28
3	4.16	4.23	4.16	4.21
4	4.11	3.98	4.20	4.04
1955				
1	4.23	4.19	3.86	4.12
2	4.41	3.95	4.20	4.24
3	4.43	4.15	4.29	4.35
4	4.55	4.68	4.43	4.61
1956				
1	4.58	4.46	4.43	4.57
2	4.66	4.53	4.65	4.64
3	4.84	4.81	4.88	4.76
4	5.21	5.28	5.20	5.13

(continued)

TABLE 32 (concluded)

Year and Quarter	C_1 (1)	C_2 (2)	C_3 (3)	C_4 (4)
1957				
1	5.38	5.58	5.21	5.36
2	5.45	5.27	5.22	5.34
3	5.72	6.36	5.65	5.63
4	5.66	5.95	5.79	5.63
1958				
1	5.44	5.45	5.51	5.36
2	5.33	5.30	5.16	5.16
3	5.24	5.49	5.08	5.22
4	5.58	5.47	5.32	5.41
1959				
1	5.67	6.05	5.76	5.59
2	5.73	5.50	5.52	5.62
3	5.84	5.38	5.82	5.74
4	6.11	5.72	5.75	6.05
1960				
1	6.15	6.18	5.33	6.02
2	6.01	5.30	5.88	5.93
3	6.07	5.42	6.03	5.92
4	5.81	6.12	5.82	5.86
1961				
1	5.87	5.66	5.53	5.84
2	5.64	5.49	5.50	5.63
3	5.79	5.70	5.77	5.89
4	5.65	5.50	5.71	5.61

Source: Col. 1, see Table 28, column 4; col. 2, see Table 30, column 4; col. 3, computed at 1956 mean values for ten significant variables given in Table 31; col. 4, arithmetic average over all actual yields on industrials in sample.

Two additional composite series for industrials were also obtained.

For the first, the three computed series were simply averaged arithmetically (Column 4 of Table 30 and Column 2 of Table 32).

Second, a composite computed series was obtained by using

CHART 12

Industrials: Three Composite Yield Series Compared with Each Other and with Movements of Yields on Long-Term Governments, Quarterly, 1951–61

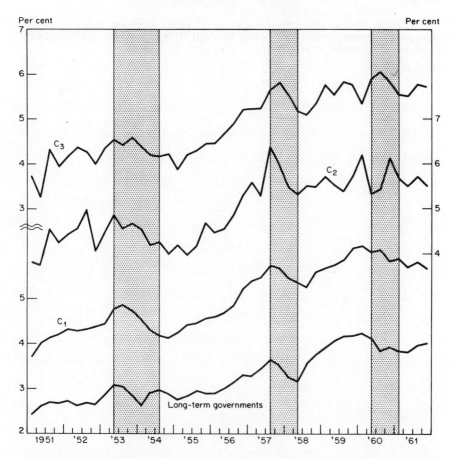

Shaded areas represent business contractions; white areas, expansions.
SOURCE: Table 32 and *Treasury Bulletin.*

mean values for the significant variables for 1956—the midyear of
the period (Table 31). The forty-four regression equations (given
by the rerun on the significant variables) were evaluated at these
mean values. This series is given in column 3 of Table 32.

All three series are compared in Chart 12. The composite cross-
classified series and the computed series based on 1956 mean
values are closest together and both conform fairly closely to
NBER turning points in business cycles. The arithmetic average
of the three computed series (C_2) shows five or six erratic movements.[25]

[25] Whether the "fixed characteristics" series really represent constant quality
remains to be seen. This problem will be dealt with in the study of the quality
of direct placements, at present under way.

4

YIELDS ON PUBLIC UTILITIES

Public utilities differ in one primary respect from industrial companies: nearly all of them dispense first-order necessities, enjoy legal monopolies, and are subject much less than industrial companies to the changes in fortune brought about by the development of new products. In brief, public utilities are more stable than industrial companies and in general are so regarded by lenders.

For this reason lenders tend to be much more lenient with utilities than with industrial companies. They require typically that only 2 to 5 per cent of any given loan be amortized over its life— the expectation being that, at maturity, the outstanding balance will be refinanced.[1]

As a result, the average term of the typical utility tends to be much longer, relative to maturity, than the average term of the typical industrial loan. This, in turn, means that the typical utility will need less cash than an industrial company to make the required payments on a loan of any given size. For this reason, lenders generally do not require nearly as much coverage for a loan to a utility as for a loan to an industrial company.

In general the procedures used in this chapter are the same as those used in Chapter 3 for industrials. First, the variables checked in column 2 of Table 13 were tested to obtain the relevant variables. These are given in Table 33 together with their regression coefficients and the percentage impact of each on yield.

The most important variables, as Table 33 indicates, were X_{4r}, X_2, X_3, and X_{12}. In order to maintain conformity with the cross-

---

[1] Gas transmission companies, which have been classified here as utilities, are an exception to this generalization.

TABLE 33

*Public Utilities: Significant Variables, Their Regression
Coefficients and Percentage Impact on Yield*

Variable	Regression Coefficient	Percentage Impact on Yield
X_2	−.0675	12
X_3	−.1355	5
X_{4r}	+.0830	15
X_5	+.0132	1
X_6	−.0105	1
X_7	+.0033	1
X_8	−.0099	1
X_{12}	−.0237	4
X_{13}	+.0644	2
X_{15}	−.0253	1

classified series on industrials, X_4 in its original form (coverage) and X_2 were used to construct the cross-classified series for utilities. A trade-off was found between these two variables, class intervals were established, and the original observations cross classified accordingly (Table 46 and Chart 14).

Mean values for each variable were obtained, as for industrials, and yields *computed* for each class quarterly (Table 47). The final computed series themselves are given in Table 46 and in Chart 14. The computed series are compared with their cross-classified counterparts in Chart 15.

A composite series was then computed, analogous to the computed composite series for industrials (Table 48). It is compared with yields on FHA mortgages and long-term governments in Chart 16.

Finally, both cross-classified and computed series were constructed for electric and telephone companies and for water and gas distribution companies. These series are given in Table 50 and in Chart 18.

Variables and Form of Function

The variables used to analyze utility issues are identical to those used to analyze industrial issues with one exception—the ratio of working capital to long-term debt (X_{14}). This ratio is not considered to be of any importance by many lenders and data on it were therefore often not available. The same initial form of function was used to analyze utility issues as was used to analyze industrial issues.[2]

THE SIMPLE CORRELATIONS

Table 34 provides, in matrix form, weighted average simple correlation coefficients, Y on each X, and each X on each other X. This table indicates, for example, that the weighted average correlation of Y with X_2 over the whole period was $-.39$. The number 2 immediately below this figure indicates 2 plus signs. Correspondingly, the correlation of Y with X_3 was $-.51$ and with X_4, $-.30$ and so forth. The correlation of X_2 with X_3 was $+.17$, and so forth.

Table 35 arrays the simple correlations of Y on each X in decreasing order of size. On the whole, the simple correlations are not quite as high for utilities as they were for industrials (see Table 17). But it is perhaps worth noting that the first eight variables listed in Table 35 are identical to the first eight listed in Table 17, although they do not appear in the same order in both tables.

Tables 36 and 37 give the simple correlation coefficients by major groups: size, duration, security, variability, profitability, and growth. The size variables are all highly intercorrelated and each is moderately correlated with average term and maturity.[3] The two

[2] See above, Ch. 3.
[3] Although less so than in the case of industrials.

TABLE 34

Public Utilities: Weighted Average Correlation Coefficients, Y on Each X and Each X on Each Other X, 1951–61

	Y	X_2	X_3	X_4	X_5	X_6	X_7	X_8	X_9	X_{10}	X_{11}	X_{12}	X_{13}	X_{15}	X_{16}	X_{17}	X_{18}	X_{19}
Y	1.00																	
X_2	-.39 (2)	1.00																
X_3	-.51 (0)	+.17 (16)	1.00															
X_4	-.30 (2)	+.18 (18)	+.10 (17)	1.00														
X_5	+.20 (19)	+.14 (18)	-.33 (0)	+.07 (16)	1.00													
X_6	+.22 (20)	+.02 (10)	-.56 (0)	-.20 (4)	+.14 (15)	1.00												
X_7	+.13 (17)	-.05 (9)	+.01 (13)	-.08 (10)	+.01 (11)	-.02 (8)	1.00											
X_8	-.38 (2)	+.90 (22)	+.19 (17)	+.08 (15)	+.14 (17)	+.06 (14)	-.03 (10)	1.00										
X_9	-.11 (8)	-.04 (12)	+.08 (14)	+.27 (20)	+.05 (10)	+.05 (11)	-.02 (13)	-.02 (12)	1.00									
X_{10}	-.05 (9)	+.10 (14)	+.03 (13)	+.13 (17)	+.01 (12)	+.14 (16)	-.04 (7)	+.10 (15)	+.87 (22)	1.00								
X_{11}	+.20 (17)	-.27 (0)	-.19 (3)	-.31 (0)	-.02 (10)	+.15 (19)	-.06 (13)	-.19 (2)	-.25 (3)	-.18 (6)	1.00							
X_{12}	-.41 (2)	+.97 (22)	+.15 (17)	+.37 (20)	+.16 (18)	-.01 (10)	-.07 (8)	+.87 (22)	+.10 (13)	+.14 (15)	-.33 (0)	1.00						
X_{13}	-.43 (2)	+.17 (17)	+.87 (22)	+.11 (17)	-.31 (0)	-.50 (0)	.00 (12)	+.20 (18)	+.05 (12)	+.01 (13)	-.14 (3)	+.17 (16)	1.00					
X_{15}	+.17 (18)	+.06 (11)	-.09 (7)	-.57 (0)	+.07 (8)	+.22 (17)	-.02 (9)	+.11 (17)	-.04 (7)	+.08 (14)	+.02 (10)	-.01 (9)	-.07 (7)	1.00				
X_{16}	-.42 (2)	+.91 (22)	+.29 (20)	+.09 (16)	+.10 (17)	.00 (11)	-.03 (10)	+.99 (22)	+.03 (12)	+.10 (15)	-.20 (2)	+.86 (22)	+.25 (18)	+.09 (14)	1.00			
X_{17}	+.21 (18)	-.25 (1)	-.17 (3)	-.34 (2)	-.05 (9)	+.17 (19)	+.06 (13)	-.18 (3)	-.23 (2)	-.11 (8)	+.81 (22)	-.32 (1)	-.13 (4)	+.04 (14)	-.20 (3)	1.00		
X_{18}	-.26 (3)	+.18 (17)	+.35 (21)	+.24 (19)	-.09 (10)	-.14 (6)	.00 (8)	+.12 (16)	+.25 (16)	+.24 (14)	-.41 (0)	+.23 (17)	+.29 (21)	.00 (10)	+.16 (16)	-.34 (0)	1.00	
X_{19}	-.35 (4)	+.96 (22)	+.06 (16)	+.33 (21)	+.18 (18)	+.04 (13)	-.06 (7)	+.86 (22)	+.07 (14)	+.10 (14)	-.24 (0)	+.97 (22)	+.01 (14)	-.01 (10)	+.84 (21)	-.20 (1)	-.01 (10)	1.00

Note: Numbers in parentheses refer to number of positive relationships between the pairs of variables.

TABLE 35

*Public Utilities: Weighted Average Correlation of Yield with Each
Independent Variable, and Number of Plus Signs, 1951–61*

Variable[a]	Correlation with Yield	Number of Plus Signs
X_3	−.51	0
X_{13}	−.43	2
X_{15}	−.42	2
X_{12}	−.41	2
X_2	−.39	2
X_8	−.38	2
X_{18}	−.35	4
X_4	−.30	2
X_{17}	−.26	3
X_6	+.22	20
X_{16}	+.21	18
X_{11}	+.20	17
X_5	+.20	19
X_{15}	+.17	18
X_7	+.13	17
X_9	−.11	8
X_{10}	−.05	9

[a]Quarter of year (X_1) not included.

last variables are highly intercorrelated. Two of the security variables (X_4 and Y_{14}) are moderately intercorrelated. The third, X_5, is virtually uncorrelated with the other two. The variability variables are highly intercorrelated, as are the growth variables; the two profitability variables are only moderately so.

TABLE 36

Public Utilities: Weighted Average Correlations Among Various Size and Duration Variables, 1951–61

| | Y | Size Variables | | | | | Duration Variables | |
		X_2	X_8	X_{12}	X_{15}	X_{18}	X_3	X_{13}
Y	1.00							
X_2	-.39	1.00						
X_8	-.38	+.90	1.00					
X_{12}	-.41	+.97	+.87	1.00				
X_{16}	-.42	+.91	+.99	+.86	1.00			
X_{19}	-.35	+.96	+.86	+.97	+.84	1.00		
X_3	-.51	+.17	+.19	+.15	+.29	+.06	1.00	
X_{13}	-.43	+.17	+.20	+.17	+.25	+.01	+.87	1.00

TABLE 37

Public Utilities: Weighted Average Correlations Within Various Classes of Independent Variables, 1951–61

Financial Security

	Y	X_4	X_5	X_{14}
X_4	-.30	1.00		
X_5	+.20	+.07	1.00	
X_{15}	+.17	-.57	+.07	1.00

Variability

	Y	X_{11}	X_{16}
X_{11}	+.20	1.00	
X_{17}	+.21	+.81	1.00

Profitability

	Y	X_{12}	X_{17}
X_{12}	-.41	1.00	
X_{18}	-.26	+.23	1.00

Growth

	Y	X_9	X_{10}
X_9	-.11	1.00	
X_{10}	-.05	+.87	1.00

TABLE 38

Public Utilities: Twenty-Two Regressions, Yield on Eighteen Variables, R^2, F, Probability of F, Degrees of Freedom, Semiannually, 1951–61

	R^2	F	$P_F \lessgtr$	Degrees of Freedom
1951				
1	.925	3.1	a	4
2	.835	3.9	.01	14
1952				
1	.806	1.8	a	7
2	.584	0.9	a	12
1953				
1	.839	2.0	a	7
2	.449	0.8	a	18
1954				
1	.895	6.2	.01	13
2	.903	9.3	.01	18
1955				
1	.832	5.2	.01	19
2	.803	3.2	.05	14
1956				
1	.912	3.4	a	6
2	.766	3.4	a	19
1957				
1	.805	5.1	.01	22
2	.828	7.3	.01	27
1958				
1	.650	2.6	.05	25
2	.591	1.8	a	22
1959				
1	.753	2.7	.05	16
2	.949	2.1	a	2
1960				
1	.850	7.9	.01	25
2	.964	7.5	.05	5
1961				
1	.832	8.00	.01	29
2	.980	3.1	a	1

[a] P_F greater than .05.

TABLE 39

Public Utilities: Significance of Each Variable, $X_2 - X_{19}$, When that Variable Was Introduced into Regression, Semiannually, 1951–61

		t_{X_2}	t_{X_3}	t_{X_4}	t_{X_5}	t_{X_6}	t_{X_7}	t_{X_8}	t_{X_9}	$t_{X_{10}}$
1951										
	1	−1.44	−1.42	+0.35	−0.77	−0.95	−0.70	+0.21	+0.60	+1.12
	2	−3.57	−3.96	−0.89	+2.06	−2.51	+0.51	−0.47	+1.02	−0.02
1952										
	1	−2.17	−2.55	−1.56	−0.21	−1.08	−0.60	+0.52	−0.36	+0.61
	2	+0.88	−0.23	+1.01	+0.92	+1.69	+1.39	+1.35	+1.09	−0.67
1953										
	1	−0.41	−4.81	−0.19	+2.07	+1.47	+3.11	+0.36	+0.51	−0.12
	2	+1.06	−2.04	−2.20	−0.29	−0.14	+0.64	+0.07	+0.07	+0.13
1954										
	1	−3.30	−2.92	−2.29	−1.44	−1.48	+0.16	+3.33	−1.07	−2.07
	2	−5.61	−2.00	−1.53	+3.30	+2.01	−0.42	−0.12	−1.99	+1.31
1955										
	1	−1.57	−7.67	−2.77	−0.21	−0.61	−0.27	−1.31	−0.93	−0.97
	2	−4.72	−3.76	−1.47	−0.70	−0.07	+0.88	+0.42	+0.57	−0.16
1956										
	1	−1.41	−2.86	−1.68	+2.18	−0.47	+1.51	+0.98	+0.28	+1.49
	2	−3.64	−5.16	−1.37	−0.39	−0.98	+0.42	+0.81	−0.10	−0.71
1957										
	1	−0.77	−7.25	+0.91	+2.15	−3.40	+1.61	−1.16	+0.94	−0.03
	2	−4.88	−3.29	−2.50	−0.59	−2.02	+1.79	−3.33	+1.00	−1.08
1958										
	1	−0.98	−4.60	−3.14	+0.67	−1.36	+0.61	−2.40	+0.13	+1.28
	2	−1.63	−2.70	−1.83	+0.00	−1.24	+0.36	−1.28	−0.69	+0.34
1959										
	1	−4.23	−1.54	−2.38	+0.82	+1.03	−1.39	−3.22	+0.01	+0.40
	2	−2.60	−3.03	−0.92	+1.27	−1.16	+1.62	−0.63	+0.68	−1.62
1960										
	1	−3.93	−3.67	−2.99	+3.25	−1.29	−1.25	−1.13	−0.95	+1.44
	2	−5.35	−2.95	−1.24	+1.99	−0.95	+2.00	+0.58	+0.96	+1.70
1961										
	1	−3.93	−4.34	−1.86	+1.47	−0.26	+0.59	−3.70	+2.09	+2.07
	2	−4.31	−0.88	−2.43	+1.28	−1.94	−0.65	−0.97	−1.96	+0.20
$\bar{t}$		−2.66	−3.35	−1.50	+0.86	−0.71	−0.54	−0.55	−0.01	+0.21

(continued)

TABLE 39 (concluded)

	$_tX_{11}$	$_tX_{12}$	$_tX_{13}$	$_tX_{15}$	$_tX_{16}$	$_tX_{17}$	$_tX_{18}$	$_tX_{19}$
1951								
1	+0.15	+0.36	+2.81	+0.47	-0.43	+2.80	---	---
2	-2.07	+1.24	+1.74	-0.74	+0.19	+0.33	+1.24	+0.38
1952								
1	+0.17	+2.16	+1.08	-1.02	-1.44	+0.06	---	---
2	-1.34	+0.79	+0.72	+1.07	+0.25	+0.31	+1.09	-0.54
1953								
1	-0.48	+1.23	-0.06	-0.54	-1.13	+0.44	-0.25	-0.49
2	-0.45	-0.58	+1.67	+0.21	-0.58	+0.55	+0.88	+0.05
1954								
1	-0.35	+1.17	+1.95	-1.32	-1.09	-1.61	+1.12	-0.06
2	+1.17	+1.14	+3.45	-2.54	+0.91	- .13	+0.56	+0.46
1955								
1	+1.01	+0.84	-0.53	-1.69	+0.59	-1.12	-1.40	+0.84
2	+0.89	+1.69	-0.66	-1.48	+0.85	-0.14	-0.03	+1.51
1956								
1	-1.21	+0.47	+0.22	-1.24	-0.97	-1.83	-1.54	+1.35
2	-0.27	+0.61	+0.55	-0.48	-0.41	+0.91	-0.20	+0.43
1957								
1	-1.51	+0.68	+0.28	+0.59	+0.58	+0.25	-0.54	+0.19
2	+0.20	+1.92	-1.24	+1.33	-2.14	+0.29	-0.94	+0.40
1958								
1	+0.32	-0.92	+0.47	+0.31	-0.29	+0.55	+0.71	+0.43
2	-0.52	+0.73	-1.85	-2.29	+0.82	+0.98	+0.12	+0.80
1959								
1	-0.72	-0.32	+1.39	+0.62	-0.21	-0.27	-0.70	-0.63
2	-0.40	-0.09	+0.17	-0.68	-0.56	+1.67	-0.22	-1.25
1960								
1	-1.83	+2.14	-0.04	+2.68	+0.76	-0.49	-1.64	-0.80
2	-0.00	+0.12	-3.91	+0.03	+0.56	+0.50	-0.95	-0.82
1961								
1	-0.11	-0.37	+0.56	+3.61	-0.38	+1.06	-0.70	+1.41
2	+0.37	-0.02	+2.40	-1.09	-0.95	-0.18	---	---
$\bar{t}$	-0.32	+0.68	+0.51	-0.20	-0.23	+0.22	-0.18	+0.28

See note a, Table 21.

THE STEPWISE REGRESSIONS

Next, twenty-two stepwise regressions were run, one for each of the twenty-two half years in 1951–61. As indicated above, the form of function used was identical to that used for industrials. Table 38 gives results, for the final equation, for each of these twenty-two cross sections: R^2, F, probability of F, and degrees of freedom. On the whole, the results are satisfactory, i.e., in most cross sections, the hypothesis used explains a large percentage of the variation in yield. In six cross sections R^2 is greater than .90; in sixteen, greater than .80.[4]

The Significant Variables

As in Chapter 3, the first step was to determine which variables show statistical significance when entered into the regression. For this purpose, the same three tests were used as for industrials: a t̄ test, a sign test, and a distribution of 't's' test. If any variable showed significance by any one of these three tests, it was presumed to be significant when entered into the regression.[5]

Tables 39, 40, and 41 respond to the question of "significance when entered." Tables 39 and 40 suggest three conclusions.

1. Of the eighteen variables, only two (X_2 and X_3) show consistently high t's over the twenty-two cross sections.

2. Two additional variables, X_4 and X_5, show distributions which are markedly skewed in one direction or the other. Eight of the twenty-two t's for X_4 (36.4 per cent) are equal to or less than −2.00, and six of the twenty-two t's for X_5 (27.3 per cent) are equal to or greater than +2.00. One variable, X_{15}, shows 18.2 per cent of the t's in the tails—albeit equally divided between both.

---

[4] In most of the twenty-two cross sections, F would have been materially increased and R^2 not materially reduced had the last eight or ten variables not been used.

[5] For the purpose at hand, conservative procedure requires that mistakes, if any, should be in the direction of classifying "uncertain" variables as being significant.

TABLE 40

*Public Utilities: $\bar{t}$'s and Distribution of t's, When Entered,
Partial Regression Coefficients on $X_2 - X_{19}$*

Coefficient	$\bar{t}$	Per Cent $\bar{\leq}-2.00$	Per Cent $\bar{\geq}+2.00$
b_2	-2.66	59.1	--
b_3	-3.35	77.3	--
b_4	-1.50	36.4	--
b_5	-0.86	-- .	27.3
b_6	-0.71	13.6	4.5
b_7	-0.54	--	9.1
b_8	-0.55	18.2	4.5
b_9	-0.01	--	4.5
b_{10}	+0.21	4.5	4.5
b_{11}	-0.32	4.5	--
b_{12}	+0.68	--	9.1
b_{13}	+0.51	4.5	13.6
b_{15}	-0.20	9.1	9.1
b_{16}	-0.23	4.5	--
b_{17}	+0.22	--	4.5
b_{18}	-0.18	--	--
b_{19}	+0.28	--	--

3. One other variable, X_8, shows skewness but not as much as the others: four of the twenty-two t's (18.2 per cent) are equal to or less than −2.00.

Table 41 gives the results of the sign test on each variable when that variable was entered into the regression. It shows, for example, that the sign of the coefficient on X_2 was positive twice and negative twenty times in twenty-two regressions, and that the sign of the coefficient on X_3 was negative twenty-two times. By this test, two

TABLE 41

Public Utilities: *Number of Plus and Minus Signs Obtained
on Partial Regression Coefficients and Binomial Probability of
Obtaining at Least Larger Number if Actual Probability is .50*

Coefficient	No. of Plus Signs	No. of Minus Signs	$P_B \lessgtr$
b_2	2	20	.000
b_3	0	22	.000
b_4	3	19	.000
b_5	14	8	.143
b_6	4	18	.002
b_7	15	7	.067
b_8	10	12	.416
b_9	13	9	.262
b_{10}	12	10	.416
b_{11}	8	14	.143
b_{12}	16	6	.026
b_{13}	15	7	.067
b_{15}	9	13	.262
b_{16}	9	13	.262
b_{17}	13	9	.262
b_{18}[a]	7	12	.180
b_{19}[a]	13	6	.084

[a]Insufficient degrees of freedom in three cross sections.

additional variables are presumed to be clearly significant (X_6 and X_{12}) and two marginally so (X_7 and X_{13}).

Trends were then fitted to those coefficients which had not otherwise shown significance (b_9, b_{10}, b_{11}, b_{16}, b_{17}, b_{18}, b_{19}), and also to b_{15}, which had behaved, when entered, in a somewhat ambiguous way. None of these coefficients showed trend, except b_{15} which showed strong trend ($P < .01$). Thus, we may presume that, in the absence of trend, X_{15} would probably have shown significance by the sign test or by the distribution of t's test, or both.[6]

Last, each of the seven variables which had shown no significance when entered, was examined in the light of subsequent variables. None showed significance as variables were added.

RERUN ON SIGNIFICANT VARIABLES

In order to determine whether all ten variables were independently significant, the regressions were rerun, semiannually,[7] with X_4 redefined (as for industrials). Quarter of year was added as a dummy variable in order to hold constant within each half year some of the effects of time. Table 42 gives R^2, F, and degrees of freedom for each of these twenty-two regressions. As we would expect, R^2 has been reduced (see Table 38). The size of the cross section has not been narrowed (as it was when industrials were rerun) but seven variables have been eliminated. On the other hand, 70 per cent or more of the variation in yield is being explained in sixteen of the twenty-two cross sections, and the statistical significance of the results has materially increased. Sixteen of the twenty-two F's are now significant at .01 or better, whereas only eight were significant when the regressions were run on eighteen variables.

The presumption is that had it been possible to narrow the cross section to three months, R^2 would not have been materially reduced and might, indeed, have been increased. This presumption was tested by running regressions for those quarters in which degrees of freedom ≥ 10. This test produced R^2 as follows: (1) third and fourth quarters of 1956 equaled .733 and .891, respectively, compared with .766 for the second half of 1956 with eighteen variables included; (2) first and second quarters of 1957 equaled .878 and .929, respectively, compared with .805 for the first half of 1957 with eighteen variables included; (3) first and second quarters of

[6] In any event, a coefficient cannot show trend unless it exists!

[7] They could not be rerun quarterly because not enough observations were available in some quarters.

TABLE 42

Public Utilities: Twenty-Two Regressions, Yield on Eleven
Variables, R^2, F, Probability of F, Degrees of Freedom,
Semiannually, 1951–61

	R^2	F	$P_{F \gtrless}$	Degrees of Freedom
1951				
1	.672	1.7	a	11
2	.745	5.6	.01	21
1952				
1	.664	2.2	a	14
2	.445	1.4	a	19
1953				
1	.797	5.0	.01	14
2	.384	1.4	a	25
1954				
1	.783	6.5	.01	20
2	.841	12.0	.01	25
1955				
1	.766	7.7	.01	26
2	.706	4.6	.01	21
1956				
1	.663	2.3	a	13
2	.750	7.1	.01	26
1957				
1	.789	9.9	.01	29
2	.781	10.7	.01	34
1958				
1	.623	4.8	.01	32
2	.549	3.2	.05	29
1959				
1	.733	5.7	.01	23
2	.767	2.7	a	9
1960				
1	.814	12.7	.01	32
2	.941	17.3	.01	12
1961				
1	.799	13.0	.01	36
2	.941	8.6	.01	8

[a]P_F is greater than .05.

1958 equaled .710 and .650, respectively, compared with .650 for the first half of 1958 with eighteen variables included; (4) first and second quarters of 1961 equaled .916 and .915, respectively, compared with .832 for the first half of 1961 with eighteen variables included. These four comparisons were the only ones which could be made, but they provided some evidence that R^2 would have been very high had it been possible to narrow the cross section from six to three months.

Table 43 assesses the performance of each significant variable in the reruns. By the distribution of "t's" test (columns 1 and 2 of Table 43), all ten coefficients show a larger number of high or low

TABLE 43

Public Utilities: Twenty-Two Regressions, Yield on Eleven Variables, Number of Times t Was Greater Than +2.00 or Less Than −2.00 and Distribution of Plus and Minus Signs of Coefficients

Coefficients	t Greater Than +2.00	t Less Than −2.00	Distribution of Signs		$P_{B} \gtreqless$
			Plus	Minus	
b_2	0	3	7	15	.067
b_3	0	10	0	22	.000
b_{4r}	6	0	17	5	.01
b_5	3	0	16	6	.026
b_6	0	2	5	17	.01
b_7	2	1	14	8	.143
b_8	1	6	10	12	.000
b_{12}	0	5	8	14	.143
b_{13}	3	1	16	6	.026
b_{15}	2	2	9	13	.262

See notes to Table 25.

t's than would be expected on the basis of chance alone—although b_6 is marginal. Of the ten coefficients, all but three also showed significance by the sign test, although b_2 was marginal.

IMPORTANCE OF VARIABLES

The question now is: Which of the foregoing ten variables are capable of exerting a substantial effect on yield? To determine this, an over-all regression was run with X_4 redefined as was done for industrials. Results are given in Table 44. Using the regression

TABLE 44

Public Utilities: "Over-All" Regression, Log Y on Eleven Variables, Regression Coefficients, Standard Errors, and Tests of Significance

Coefficient	$\bar{b}$	$\sigma_{\bar{b}}$	t	$P_{t \lessgtr}^{a}$
Intercept	+.9710	.0795	+12.21	.001
b_1	+.8872	.0210	+42.32	.001
b_2	−.0675	.0173	− 3.91	.001
b_3	−.1355	.0153	− 8.84	.001
b_{4r}	+.0830	.0163	+ 5.09	.001
b_5	+.0132	.0036	+ 3.62	.001
b_6	−.0105	.0053	− 1.99	.05
b_7	+.0033	.0007	+ 4.85	.001
b_8	−.0099	.0042	− 2.33	.02
b_{12}	−.0237	.0069	− 3.43	.001
b_{13}	+.0644	.0205	+ 3.15	.01
b_{15}	−.0253	.0192	− 1.32	.20

[a]With 725 degrees of freedom, two tailed.

For this regression, R^2 = .856, F = 388.3, and $P_{F \lessgtr}$ = .001.

TABLE 45

Public Utilities: Percentage Impact of Each Variable on Yield
When that Variable Increased by One Standard Deviation

Variable	b_i (1)	σ_{x_i} (2)	$b_i\,\sigma_{x_i}$ (3)	Antilog of Col. 3[a] (4)
X_2	−.0675	1.6583	−.11194	1.12
X_3	−.1355	.3684	−.04992	1.05
X_{4r}	+.0830	1.6520	+.13712	1.15
X_5	+.0132	.7736	+.01021	1.01
X_6	−.0105	.6060	−.00636	1.01
X_7	+.0033	4.2685	+.01409	1.01
X_8	−.0099	1.4487	−.01434	1.01
X_{12}	−.0237	1.7523	−.04153	1.04
X_{13}	+.0644	.2535	+.01633	1.02
X_{15}	−.0253	.2153	−.00545	1.01

[a]Signs ignored.

coefficients from this over-all regression, the percentage impact of each variable was calculated. Results are given in Table 45. Ranked in the order of their importance in this sense, the variables appear in much the same order for utilities as for industrials (X_{4r}, X_2, X_3, X_{12}, X_{13}, X_8, X_7, X_5, X_6, X_{15}).[8]

The Cross-Classified Series

As the first step in constructing a cross-classified series for public utilities, quarterly regressions were run on X_2 and X_4, as for in-

---

[8] X_{15}, which was deemed significant in the cross sections, showed only slight significance over all. But see Chart D-2.

CHART 13

*Public Utilities: System of Cross Classification Used to
Construct Eight Cross-Classified Yield Series, 1951–61*

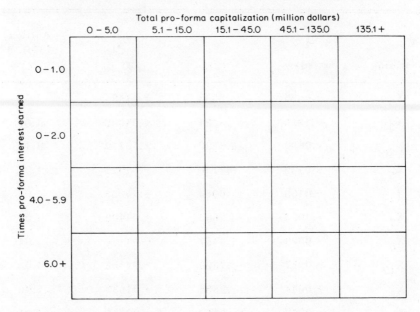

Total pro-forma capitalization (million dollars)

dustrials. Weighted averages were then struck over the forty-four coefficients on X_2 and the forty-four coefficients on X_4. These averages were, respectively, $-.0210$ and $-.0437$.[9]

With these weighted average coefficients in hand, class intervals were established for X_2 and X_4 such that the sum $b_2 \log X_2 + b_4 \log X_4$ (the X values taken at the mean value of each class interval) was approximately the same along each left-to-right diagonal.

The class intervals used (Chart 13) differ from the class-intervals used for industrials (Chart 6) primarily because the range of X_4 is much narrower for utilities than for industrials.

As for industrials, averages were obtained over the observations lying along each left-to-right diagonal. This procedure produced eight basic series, which were consolidated into three classes by

[9] Neither coefficient showed any trend over the period. Both showed a high degree of significance. The t for b_2 was -10.91 ($P_t = .001$) and for b_4, -6.56 ($P_t = .001$).

TABLE 46

Public Utilities: Yields on Direct Placements, Cross Classified and Computed, by Class, Quarterly, 1951–61

Year and Quarter	Cross Classified[a]		Computed	
	Class I	Class II	Class I	Class II
1951				
1	3.47	3.34[b]	3.68	3.49[b]
2	3.53	4.00	3.68	3.48[b]
3	3.57	4.20	3.74	3.98
4	3.74	3.94	3.80	4.04
1952				
1	3.52	3.81	3.59	3.53[b]
2	3.76	3.91	3.55	3.48[b]
3	3.98	3.75[b]	3.21	3.41
4	3.54	4.10	3.33	3.53
1953				
1	4.15	4.00[b]	3.93	4.22
2	3.92	4.13	4.15	4.45
3	4.21	4.38	4.12	4.31
4	4.26	4.03[b]	3.87	4.05
1954				
1	3.49	3.92	3.64	3.82
2	3.45	4.10	3.62	3.78
3	3.25	4.25	3.80	3.91
4	3.42	4.04	3.69	3.79
1955				
1	3.84	4.13	3.65	3.84
2	3.58	4.00	3.76	3.96
3	3.65	3.97	3.75	3.94
4	3.80	4.22	3.78	3.97
1956				
1	4.03	3.88[b]	3.98	4.10
2	4.09	4.33	4.24	4.36
3	4.50	4.75	4.45	4.63
4	4.88	5.04	4.77	4.96

(continued)

TABLE 46 (concluded)

Year and Quarter	Cross Classified[a]		Computed	
	Class I	Class II	Class I	Class II
1957				
1	5.24	5.22[b]	5.03	5.26
2	4.98	5.05	4.96	5.19
3	5.33	5.95	5.20	5.39
4	5.26	5.50	5.13	5.32
1958				
1	4.47	5.21	4.41	4.95
2	4.72	5.05	4.51	5.05
3	5.26	5.16[b]	4.88	4.81[b]
4	5.00	5.62	4.99	4.93[b]
1959				
1	4.89	5.31	4.88	5.45
2	4.91	5.75	4.96	5.54
3	5.49	5.83	5.42	5.63
4	5.56	5.91	5.76	5.98
1960				
1	5.65	6.75	5.53	5.84
2	5.43	5.81	5.38	5.68
3	5.13	5.84	5.07	5.51
4	5.32	5.82	5.32	5.78
1961				
1	5.21	5.59	4.90	5.49
2	5.24	5.60	4.96	5.56
3	5.00	5.62	4.99	5.30
4	4.86	5.25	4.86	5.16

[a]Cross classification of original observations.

[b]Inconsistency.

CHART 14

*Public Utilities: Yields on Direct Placements, Classes I
and II Compared, Cross Classified and Computed,
Quarterly, 1951–61*

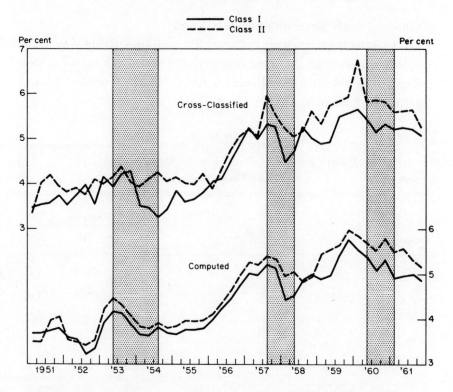

————— Class I
– – – – Class II

Cross-Classified

Computed

Shaded areas represent business contractions; white areas, expansions.
SOURCE: Table 46.

combining series 1, 2, and 3 into class I, series 4, 5, and 6 into
class II, and series 7 and 8 into class III. The number of observations in class I was small [10] and the number of inconsistencies remained relatively large. Therefore, classes I and II were thrown
together, thus reducing the number of series to two (columns 1
and 2 of Table 46 and Chart 14). The three original series were

[10] Ninety for the forty-four quarters out of about 800 observations in total.

then averaged to obtain a composite series based on the original data (column 1 of Table 48 and Chart 16).

The Computed Series

Computed series were obtained as follows:

1. Quarterly means were obtained for each underlying significant variable for each of the three consolidated series. These were then averaged to obtain over-all means, for each series separately and for each significant variable (Table 47).

TABLE 47

Public Utilities: Mean Values Used to Obtain
Computed Series, by Class

Variable	Units	Series IC	IIC	IIIC
X_2	Million dollars	121.5	15.5	4.3
X_3	Years	23.2	20.4	18.4
X_{4r}	Million dollars	2.1	0.4	0.1
X_5	a	0.3	0.4	0.2
X_6	b	1.3	1.4	1.6
X_7	Years	2.9	3.3	3.7
X_8	Million dollars	9.5	1.9	0.9
X_{12}	Million dollars	9.1	1.6	0.2
X_{13}	Years	26.9	24.8	23.1
X_{15}	Dollars of long-term debt per dollar of total capital	.49	.51	.58

[a]See note a, Table 29.

[b]For industrial classification, electric utilities and telephone companies = 1, water and gas distribution companies = 2, gas pipeline companies = 3, urban transport = 4, and "other" = 5. The figures here are an average of these code numbers.

CHART 15

CHART 15

*Public Utilities: Cross-Classified Yield Series Compared
with Computed Yield Series, by Class, Quarterly,
1951–61*

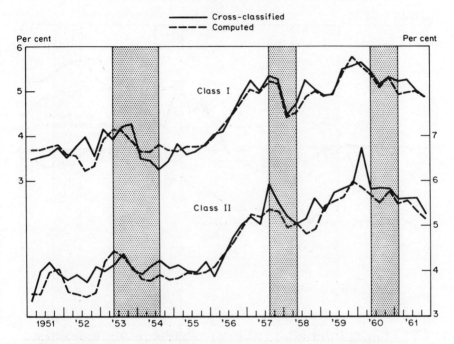

Shaded areas represent business contractions; white areas, expansions.
SOURCE: Table 46.

2. The over-all mean values were then held rigidly constant
and quarterly series were computed using the original semi-annual
regression equations obtained from the "rerun." [11]

The series for classes I and II were then averaged. The two resulting *computed* series are given in columns 3 and 4 of Table 46.
Chart 15 compares these computed series with their cross-classified
counterparts.

The three computed series were averaged to obtain a second
composite series for utilities (column 2 of Table 48 and Chart 17).

A third composite series was obtained by computation, using

[11] Quarterly values were obtained by using the coefficients obtained for each
half-year on quarter of the year.

CHART 16

Public Utilities: Yields on Direct Placements, Composite Cross Classified Compared with Yields on FHA Mortgages and Yields on Long-Term Governments, Quarterly, 1951–61

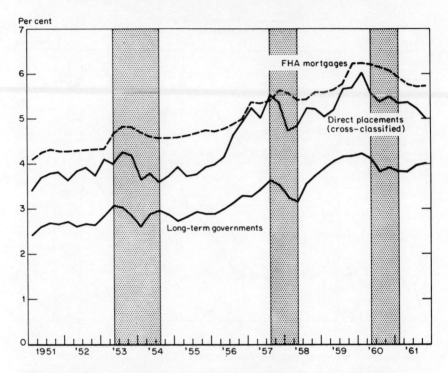

Shaded areas represent business contractions; white areas, expansions.
SOURCE: Table 48; *Federal Reserve Bulletin; Treasury Bulletin.*

1956 mean values for the X's (Table 49) and the regression equations given by the second rerun. This series thus holds all variables rigidly constant at their 1956 mean values (column 3 of Table 47 and Chart 17).

Additional Series

Various additional series for utilities were constructed.

1. Series based on *the original observations* were constructed for electric utilities and telephone companies together and water

TABLE 48

*Public Utilities: Three Composite Yield Series Compared with
Each Other and with Average Actual Yields in Sample,
Quarterly, 1951–61*

Year and Quarter	C_1 (1)	C_2 (2)	C_3 (3)	C_4 (4)
1951				
1	3.40	3.62	3.62	3.37
2	3.69	3.61	3.62	3.60
3	3.78	3.82	3.98	3.85
4	3.81	3.88	4.05	3.81
1952				
1	3.62	3.57	3.59	3.62
2	3.84	3.52	3.55	3.79
3	3.91	3.28	4.15	3.92
4	3.73	3.40	4.32	3.71
1953				
1	4.10	4.02	4.21	4.08
2	3.99	4.24	4.43	4.00
3	4.26	4.19	4.27	4.21
4	4.18	3.93	4.01	4.01
1954				
1	3.63	3.70	3.76	3.72
2	3.78	3.67	3.73	3.60
3	3.59	3.84	3.92	3.67
4	3.73	3.72	3.80	3.58
1955				
1	3.94	3.71	3.82	3.69
2	3.72	3.83	3.94	3.79
3	3.76	3.82	3.91	3.90
4	3.94	3.85	3.93	4.01
1956				
1	3.98	4.02	4.11	4.06
2	4.15	4.28	4.37	4.19
3	4.63	4.51	4.59	4.58
4	4.93	4.84	4.92	4.96

(continued)

TABLE 48 (concluded)

Year and Quarter	C_1 (1)	C_2 (2)	C_3 (3)	C_4 (4)
1957				
1	5.24	5.11	5.13	5.15
2	5.00	5.04	5.06	5.06
3	5.53	5.26	5.38	5.48
4	5.34	5.19	5.31	5.30
1958				
1	4.72	4.59	4.75	4.62
2	4.83	4.69	4.85	4.76
3	5.23	4.85	4.94	5.06
4	5.21	4.97	5.06	5.17
1959				
1	5.03	5.07	5.22	5.01
2	5.19	5.15	5.30	5.18
3	5.66	5.49	5.53	5.55
4	5.68	5.83	5.87	5.79
1960				
1	6.02	5.63	5.79	5.71
2	5.55	5.48	5.63	5.64
3	5.37	5.22	5.36	5.53
4	5.49	5.47	5.62	5.47
1961				
1	5.34	5.10	5.28	5.29
2	5.36	5.16	5.34	5.35
3	5.21	5.10	5.25	5.15
4	4.99	4.96	5.11	4.95

Source: Col. 1, arithmetic averages of three cross-classified series; col. 2, arithmetic average of three computed series; col. 3, computed at 1956 mean values for each X; col. 4, arithmetic average over all actual yields on public utilities in sample.

CHART 17

Public Utilities: Three Composite Yield Series Compared with
Each Other, Quarterly, 1951–61

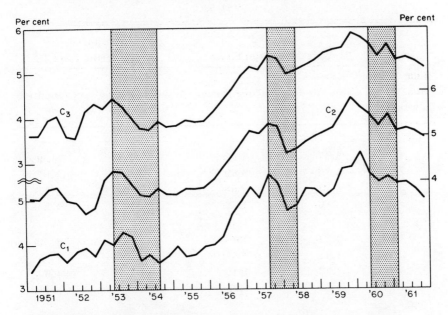

Shaded areas represent business contractions; white areas, expansions.
SOURCE: Table 48.

TABLE 49

Public Utilities: Mean Values Used To
Obtain Computed Composite Series

Variable	Units	Value
X_2	Million dollars	11.7
X_3	Years	18.5
X_{4r}	Million dollars	0.3
X_5	a	.40
X_6	b	1.6
X_7	Years	3.9
X_8	Million dollars	1.5
X_{12}	Million dollars	0.7
X_{13}	Years	23.6
X_{15}	Dollars of long-term debt per dollar of total capital	.55

[a]See note a, Table 29.
[b]See note b, Table 47.

TABLE 50

Electric and Telephone, and Water and Gas Distribution Direct Placements, Cross-Classified and Computed Yield Series, Quarterly, 1951-61

Year and Quarter	Electric and Telephone		Water and Gas Distribution	
	Cross Classified (1)	Computed (2)	Cross Classified (3)	Computed (4)
1951				
1	3.47	3.67	3.25	3.99
2	3.70	3.69	3.79	4.01
3	3.71	3.65	4.00	4.15
4	3.80	3.72	3.93	4.24
1952				
1	3.59	3.70	3.82	4.36
2	3.81	3.68	3.80	4.33
3	3.93	4.10	3.95	4.94
4	3.60	4.23	4.02	5.11
1953				
1	3.98	3.79	4.00	4.20
2	3.96	4.06	4.17	4.50
3	4.17	4.17	4.24	4.25
4	4.14	3.90	3.99	3.97
1954				
1	3.67	3.49	3.71	3.95
2	3.53	3.49	3.75	3.95
3	3.32	3.52	4.06	4.42
4	3.47	3.41	3.84	4.27
1955				
1	3.66	3.60	3.85	4.04
2	3.67	3.71	3.94	4.17
3	3.98	3.66	3.77	4.00
4	3.82	3.68	4.20	4.02
1956				
1	4.06	3.94	4.05	4.33
2	4.13	4.17	4.38	4.59
3	4.47	4.38	4.80	4.66
4	4.91	4.72	5.04	5.02

(continued)

TABLE 50 (concluded)

Year and Quarter	Electric and Telephone		Water and Gas Districution	
	Cross Classified (1)	Computed (2)	Cross Classified (3)	Computed (4)
1957				
1	5.00	5.07	5.36	5.22
2	5.05	5.00	5.13	5.15
3	5.52	5.27	5.63	5.54
4	5.29	5.21	5.60	5.47
1958				
1	4.54	4.52	4.90	4.64
2	4.77	4.61	4.71	4.73
3	5.16	4.77	5.05	5.37
4	5.15	4.89	5.20	5.50
1959				
1	4.99	4.87	5.13	5.12
2	5.16	4.95	5.19	5.20
3	5.41	5.45	5.65	5.50
4	5.75	5.76	5.88	5.81
1960				
1	5.56	5.47	5.90	5.77
2	5.55	5.32	5.88	5.60
3	5.50	5.02	5.66	5.43
4	5.24	5.26	5.72	5.69
1961				
1	5.18	4.88	5.50	5.12
2	5.38	4.94	5.35	5.19
3	5.07	4.90	5.29	5.28
4	5.00	4.79	4.72	5.16

CHART 18

*Electric and Telephone, and Water and Gas Distribution
Companies: Yields on Direct Placements, Cross Classified
and Computed, Quarterly, 1951–61*

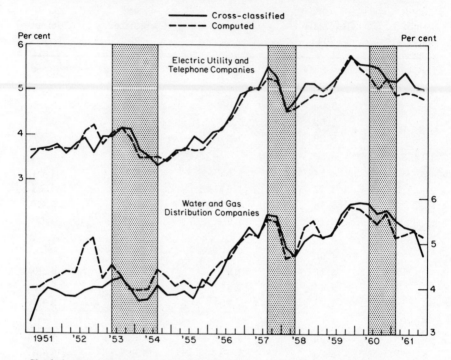

Shaded areas represent business contractions; white areas, expansions.
SOURCE: Table 50.

and gas distribution companies together. These series are given in
columns 1 and 3 of Table 50, and in Chart 18.

2. A mean value was obtained for the period *as a whole* for each
X separately for electric utilities and telephone companies, on the
one hand, and water and gas distribution companies, on the other
(Table 51). These mean values were held rigidly constant, and
quarterly series were computed separately for each type of utility
issue, using the original regression equations. These computed series
are given in columns 2 and 4 of Table 48 and in Chart 18.[12]

[12] See footnote 25, Chapter 3.

TABLE 51

*Public Utilities: Mean Values Used to Obtain Computed Series for
Electric and Telephone and Water and Gas
Distribution Placements*

		Value	
Variable	Units	Electric and Telephone	Water and Gas Distribution
X_2	Million dollars	62.4	16.6
X_3	Years	23.3	16.5
X_{4N}	Million dollars	1.2	0.5
X_5	a	0.3	0.5
X_6	b	1.0	2.0
X_7	Years	4.0	6.0
X_8	Million dollars	4.5	2.2
X_{12}	Million dollars	4.6	1.4
X_{13}	Years	27.0	22.3
X_{15}	Dollars of long-term debt per dollar of total capital	0.50	0.51

[a]See note a, Table 29.
[b]See note b, Table 47.

5

ISSUES OF FINANCE COMPANIES

Finance companies are substantially different—almost different in kind—from industrial companies and utilities. Whereas industrial companies and utilities produce and sell physical commodities and therefore hold large portions of their assets in real form, finance companies produce nothing and sell the most fungible of all commodities, money, at a time-price. In the nature of their business therefore, finance companies hold virtually no fixed assets. They hold "inventory" in the form of cash or proximate cash, and they hold notes receivable representing the time-price of the money they have sold.

Whereas the principal assets of an industrial company or a utility (i.e., their real assets) could be liquidated only by selling them (either on the basis of their value as scrap or on the basis of their potential earning power), the principal asset of finance companies, notes receivable, would liquidate itself if the company ceased doing business.[1]

For example, as of September 30, 1962, The First Southern Company, a small personal loan company, held $18.4 million in net notes receivable ($21.2 million gross, less unearned finance charges and an allowance for losses). This sum represented about 84 per cent of First Southern's total assets. On September 30, 1961, and September 30, 1960, net notes receivable represented about 75 per cent and 80 per cent, respectively, of First Southern's total assets.[2]

---

[1] This is obviously a matter of degree. The main point, of course, is that a much larger percentage of the assets of finance companies is highly liquid.

[2] At the end of 1962 all manufacturing companies held 29.8 per cent of their assets in liquid or near-liquid form. See FTC-SEC, *Quarterly Financial Report,* 4th Quarter, 1962, Table 6.

CHART 19

*Finance Companies: Actual Average Yields and Computed Yields
on Issue of Fixed Characteristics, Compared with Long-
Term Governments, Quarterly, 1951–61*

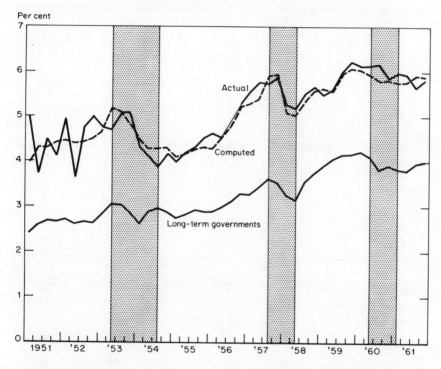

Shaded areas represent business contractions; white areas, expansions.
SOURCE: Table 60.

Only two series have been constructed for finance company
placements: "actuals," quarterly, and a computed composite series,
based on 1956 mean values for each significant variable (Table
60 and Chart 19).

Cross-classified series, by class, could not be constructed because
the total number of observations available was too small.[3] The
primary purpose of the procedures used in the chapter has been,
therefore, to isolate the significant variables [4] in order to obtain

---

[3] Less than two hundred for the entire eleven-year period.
[4] From among those checked in column 3 of Table 13.

TABLE 52

*Finance Companies: Seven Regressions, Yield on
Seventeen Variables, R^2, F, Probability of F,
Degrees of Freedom, Semiannually, 1955, 1959, 1960*

	R^2	F	$P_{F<}^=$	Degrees of Freedom
1955				
1	.949	7.4	.01	6
2	.939	8.33	.01	8
1959				
1	.817	0.30	— —	1
2	.924	6.47	.01	8
1960				
1	.640	1.42	.10	12
2	.966	1.93	— —	1
Total	.465	6.72	.01	116

regression equations which would include them alone. These regression equations (Table 55) can be used, of course, to compute yields on an issue of any desired characteristics.[5]

Preliminary Regressions

Only a small number of observations were available and therefore only six semiannual cross sections could be run on the seventeen initial variables,[6] and two of the cross sections had just one degree of freedom. Table 52 gives results (R^2, F, etc.) for these six cross sections. The R^2 for both halves of 1955 and for the second half of 1959 are very high and the corresponding F's significant at less than .01. The other three R^2's are not significant. These cross sections

---

[5] Within the range of the observations from which the regression coefficients have been derived.

[6] See column 3 of Table 10.

TABLE 53

Finance Companies: Six Semiannual Regressions, Number of Plus and Minus Signs Obtained on Partial Regression Coefficients and Binomial Probability of Obtaining at Least Larger Number if Actual Probability Is .50

Coefficient		No. of Plus Signs	No. of Minus Signs	$P_{B} \overset{=}{<}$
b_2	Total capital	3	3	.656
b_3	Average term	3	3	.656
b_4	Times charges earned	1	5	.109
b_5	Type of security	4	2	.344
b_6	Industrial class	3	3	.656
b_8	Size of issue	1	5	.109
b_9	EBIT, trend	2	4	.344
b_{12}	EBIT	4	2	.344
b_{13}	Maturity	5	1	.109
b_{17}	EBIT--coefficient of variation	5	1	.109
b_{20}	Net receivables/EBIT	3	3	.656
b_{21}	Net receivables/EBIT: trend	1	5	.109
b_{22}	Cash and receivables/total debt	3	3	.656
b_{23}	EBIT/net worth	1	5	.109
b_{24}	Net worth/senior long-term debt	2	4	.344
b_{25}	Net receivables/EBIT: coefficient of variation	0	6	.016

were run primarily to ascertain how much variation all variables together would explain when time was held approximately constant.

Next, all the observations out of the six cross sections were thrown together and one regression run on them. The R^2 (Table 52) was low largely because time was not held constant or even approximately so, but F was highly significant. All the variables which had shown significance by the sign test over the six cross sections, also showed significance when all the observations were thrown together.[7]

Of the seventeen variables tested in these initial runs, five failed to show any significance either by the sign test or by the distribution of t's test.[8] These five variables were eliminated from further consideration. They were: average term (X_3), industrial class (X_6), the ratio of cash plus receivables to total debt (X_{22}), total capital (X_2), and the ratio of net receivables to EBIT (X_{25}).

The eleven-year period was then divided into three subperiods ("cross sections"): 1951–54, 1955–57, and 1958–61. The monthly yield on Aaa corporates (Moody's) was added as a variable, in order to hold the level of interest rates constant, and four regressions were run on the remaining variables [9]—one for each of the above subperiods and one for the entire eleven-year period.

Of the twelve variables, six showed strong significance (at .01 or less) in at least one "cross section" and *all* showed significance in the over-all regression. These six variables are: monthly yield on Aaa corporates (X_1), size of issue (X_8), coefficient of variation of EBIT (X_{17}), ratio of net worth to senior long-term debt (X_{24}), type of security (X_5), and EBIT (X_{12}).

The four regressions were then rerun on these six variables, with the results given in Tables 54, 55, and 56.[10] These three tables indicate:

1. R^2 is reasonable satisfactory except for the 1958–61 cross section (Table 54).

2. The F's are high and highly significant (Table 54).

3. With the exception of the intercept and of b_{12} in 1951–54, all the cross-section coefficients decline over time (Table 55).

4. All signs, with the exception of b_5 in the 1955–57 cross section, are consistently in the expected direction (Table 56).

---

[7] By the t test at .05 or less.

[8] By "significance" is meant either four (of a possible six) signs in the same direction or one showing (of a possible six) of significance at .01 or less.

[9] Twelve variables all together, including the yield on Aaa corporates.

[10] The R^2 showed virtually no deterioration when the regressions were run on six, instead of twelve variables. See Table 57.

TABLE 54

Finance Companies: Four Regressions, Yield on Seven Variables, R^2, F, Probability of F, Degrees of Freedom, by Period, 1951-61

	R^2	F	$P_{F\leq}^<$	Degrees of Freedom
1951-54	.706	16.4	.01	41
1955-57	.857	68.7	.01	69
1958-61	.570	15.7	.01	71
1951-61	.792	124.3	.01	195

TABLE 55

Finance Companies: Regression Coefficients and Standard Errors, Four Regressions, by Period, 1951–61

Coefficient	1951–54	1955–57	1958–61	1951–61
Intercept	1.4849	.9569	1.1356	1.3482
	(.4963)	(.1401)	(.1953)	(.1018)
b_1	+1.3502	+1.1803	+ .7573	+ .8143
	(.3773)	(.0767)	(.1166)	(.0378)
b_8	− .1003	− .0320	− .0186	− .0307
	(.0276)	(.0111)	(.0084)	(.0085)
b_{17}	+ .0635	− .0280	+ .0183	+ .0278
	(.0350)	(.0175)	(.0111)	(.0107)
b_{24}	− .0716	− .0339	− .0140	− .0217
	(.0334)	(.0147)	(.0170)	(.0128)
b_5	+ .0450	+ .0251	+ .0172	+ .0307
	(.0157)	(.0087)	(.0094)	(.0072)
b_{12}	− .0015	− .0327	− .0158	− .0248
	(.0209)	(.0092	(.0071)	(.0069)

TABLE 56

Finance Companies: Expected Sign and Actual
Sign, Four Regressions, by Period,
1951–61

Coefficient	Expected Sign	Actual Sign			
		1951–54	1955–57	1958–61	1951–61
b_1	+	+	+	+	+
b_8	−	−	−	−	−
b_{17}	+	+	−	+	+
b_{24}	−	−	−	−	−
b_5	+	+	+	+	+
b_{12}	−	−	−	−	−

TABLE 57

Finance Companies: Four Regressions; R^2 with Six
Variables Compared with R^2 with Twelve Variables, by Period

No. of Variables	1951–54	1955–57	1958–61	1951–61
6	.706	.857	.570	.792
12	.726	.870	.615	.797

The importance of each coefficient was assessed by multiplying it by the standard deviation of the associated variable (Table 58). For this purpose, the coefficients and standard deviations given by the over-all regression were used.[11]

[11] The standard deviation of X_1 over the period as a whole is substantially larger than it is within any of the three cross sections. This is, of course, not true of the other variables. See Table 59.

TABLE 58

Finance Companies: Percentage Impact of Each Variable
on Yield When that Variable Increased by One Standard Deviation

Variable	b_i (1)	σ_{x_i} (2)	$b_i \sigma_{x_i}$ (3)	Antilog of Col. 3[a] (4)
X_1	+.8143	.1689	+.1375	1.12
X_8	−.0307	1.2821	−.0394	1.04
X_{17}	+.0278	.5663	+.0157	1.01
X_{24}	−.0217	.5232	−.0135	1.01
X_5	+.0307	.8947	+.0275	1.03
X_{12}	−.0248	1.5344	−.0381	1.04

[a]Signs ignored.

TABLE 59

Finance Companies: Standard Deviations of Significant
Variables, by Period, 1951–61

	1951–54	1955–57	1958–61	1951–61
X_1	.0425	.1028	.0581	.1689
X_8	1.2968	1.3427	1.2094	1.2821
X_{17}	.4539	.4455	.6207	.5663
X_{24}	.5376	.5868	.4007	.5232
X_5	.9785	.9809	.7462	.8947
X_{12}	1.7174	1.5216	1.4404	1.5344

TABLE 60

*Finance Companies: Actual Average Yields in Sample
Compared with Computed Composite Yields,
Quarterly, 1951–61*

Year and Quarter	Actual	Computed
1951		
1	5.00	3.97
2	3.71	4.33
3	4.50	4.30
4	4.10	4.43
1952		
1	4.95	4.45
2	3.62	4.39
3	4.75	4.43
4	4.99	4.51
1953		
1	4.75	4.67
2	4.70	5.19
3	5.07	5.09
4	5.06	4.79
1954		
1	4.31	4.45
2	4.10	4.29
3	3.88	4.29
4	4.17	4.30
1955		
1	3.97	4.09
2	4.18	4.17
3	4.29	4.28
4	4.53	4.31
1956		
1	4.62	4.28
2	4.53	4.54
3	––	4.81
4	5.27	5.22

(continued)

TABLE 60 (concluded)

Year and Quarter	Actual	Computed
1957		
1	5.53	5.27
2	5.75	5.39
3	5.72	5.90
4	5.89	5.92
1958		
1	5.25	5.07
2	5.17	5.03
3	5.50	5.34
4	5.66	5.57
1959		
1	5.49	5.61
2	5.59	5.56
3	6.00	5.96
4	6.22	6.06
1960		
1	6.13	6.03
2	6.13	5.93
3	6.16	5.79
4	5.84	5.80
1961		
1	5.98	5.75
2	5.93	5.76
3	5.63	5.93
4	5.81	5.89

The Yield Series

No satisfactory cross-classified series could be obtained for finance company issues simply because not enough observations were available. Therefore, only two series were constructed as follows:

1. Average actual yields, quarterly, on all issues in the sample.

2. Computed yields, using average values for the X's over the whole period and the b's given by the subperiod regressions.

These two series are given in Table 60 and in Chart 19. The X values used to obtain the computed series are given in Table 61.

TABLE 61

*Finance Companies: Mean Values Used to
Obtain Computed Composite Series*

Variable		Values
X_8	Size of Issue (million dollars)	2.9
X_{17}	Coefficient of variation of EBIT	.23
X_{24}	Net worth/senior long-term debt	.68
X_5	Type of security	2.6[a]
X_{12}	EBIT (million dollars)	2.6

[a]See note a, Table 29.

6

YIELDS ON DIRECT PLACEMENTS AND YIELDS ON PUBLIC OFFERINGS

This chapter attempts to respond to the following question: are yields on direct placements higher than, lower than, or about the same as yields on comparable public offerings?

A priori, we would expect that yields *net-to-the-issuer* [1] would be about the same for comparable issues sold at the same time—regardless of whether they were direct placements or public offerings—provided only that the issues being compared had had clear access to both markets. Why, after all, should any company sell an issue to yield 4.2 per cent in the direct placement market when comparable issues are selling in the public market to yield 4.0 per cent?

The findings here suggest that two more or less separate markets exist with perhaps some overlap: The public market has a competitive advantage with respect to the issues of the larger, better-known companies and hence tends to specialize in such issues. Yields on such issues tend to be lower in the public market. On the other hand, the direct placement market has a competitive advantage with respect to the issues of smaller, lesser-known companies and hence tends to specialize in *such* issues. Yields on these issues tend to be lower in the direct placement market.

Yields Net-to-the-Issuer

The cost of flotation of public issues is not negligible. On September 7, 1951, for example, The National Container Corporation

[1] That is, after adjustment for cost of flotation.

TABLE 62

Underwriting Costs by Quality Rating and Industrial Classification,
1951, 1956, and 1961
(in basis points)

	Quality Rating				
	Aaa	Aa	A	Baa	Ba
1951					
Industrials	— —	5.3	6.7	15.0	29.4
Public utilities	3.0	3.0	4.3	11.7	— —
1956					
Industrials	5.5	5.3	7.2	8.6	15.5
Public utilities	3.0	4.3	5.8	11.0	— —
1961					
Industrials	5.6	5.7	8.3	11.0	24.5
Public utilities	4.0	4.5	5.4	9.1	— —

sold a 4½ per cent $20 million issue, rated Baa, at a cost of flotation of 4 per cent of the offering price. This meant that National Container received 4 per cent less than $20.0 million, or $19.2 million. Interest charges of 4½ per cent on the face amount (plus, of course, repayment at maturity of the face amount) raised National Container's effective cost to 4.88 per cent, or by 38 basis points. This is an extreme case but, as Table 62 indicates, cost of flotation can make a difference in cost on issues of every size and especially on smaller issues of lesser quality. In any case, however, it seems obvious that the issuer, in choosing between a direct placement and a public offering, will compare effective yields rather than nominal yields.

In order to arrive at yields net-to-the-issuer, we should adjust not merely for the cost of flotation of public offerings but also for the cost of flotation of direct placements, and other differential costs. Unhappily, this is easier said than done. Data on the under-writing costs of public offerings are publicly available and, for the

TABLE 63

Underwriting Costs or Fees Paid to Agents,
and Other Expenses, as Per Cent of Offering
Price, by Size of Issue for Direct Placements
and Public Offerings, Selected Years, 1947–50

Size of Issue[a] (million dollars)	Underwriting Costs or Fees		Other Expenses	
	Direct Placements	Public Offerings	Direct Placements	Public Offerings
0–499	1.70	7.34	1.14	2.88
500–999	1.39	5.51	.85	3.21
1,000–2,999	.86	3.52	.54	2.09
3,000–4,999	.61	1.41	.40	1.28
5,000–9,999	.59	.88	.32	1.03
10,000–24,999	.31	.99	.25	.73
25,000 and over	.22	.72	.17	.43

Source: Securities and Exchange Commission. For years, see text.
[a]Class intervals not strictly uniform in all cases as between direct placements and public offerings.

period since January 1, 1951, have been put into convenient form by Halsey, Stuart and Company.[2] But data on fees paid to agents by issuers in connection with the sale of direct placements and data on the other expenses of both types of issues are not systematically available.[3] The Securities and Exchange Commission has made estimates for three years for direct placements (1947, 1949, and 1950) and for five years for public offerings (1945–49).[4]

The pertinent figures are reproduced in Table 63. Two things are clear: first, the differential in favor of direct placements is large,

[2] See *Competitive Sales and Negotiated Public Offerings of New Public Utility, Railroad and Industrial Debt Issues,* Chicago (undated).

[3] Other expenses include listing fees, federal revenue stamps, state taxes and fees, trustee fees, printing and engraving, legal fees, accounting fees, engineering fees.

[4] Securities and Exchange Commission, *Privately-Placed Securities—Cost of Flotation* (corrected printing), Washington, D.C., September 1952.

especially on the smaller issues; for a company considering an issue of less than $500 thousand dollars, the total cost (underwriting plus other expense) averaged 10.22 per cent of offering price for a public offering (7.34 plus 2.88) but only about 3 per cent for a direct placement.[5] The difference (7 percentage points on a fifteen-year, 4 per cent issue) is equal to about 65 basis points. Although the difference on large issues is considerably less, it is not negligible; even when a fee was paid to an agent on a direct placement, the difference was about 7 basis points for issues of over $10 million and about 5 basis points for issues of over $25 million.

Second, Table 63 suggests that for every size of issue the *difference* in "other expenses," in favor of direct placements, was roughly the same as the fee paid to an agent in connection with a direct placement. Thus, in the smallest class the difference in "other expenses," 1.74 (= 2.88 − 1.14), is almost equal to the fees paid to agents. In the largest class the difference was .26 (= .43 − .17), about equal to the fees paid in that class. The relationship is rough and it is not uniform from class to class but it enables us to disregard fees paid on direct placements and other expenses on both types of issues; i.e., it enables us to put both types of issues on a comparable, net-cost-to-the-issuer basis simply by adjusting yields on public offerings for underwriting expense.[6]

The principal defect in the foregoing assumption is that fees were paid on only about half of the direct placements surveyed by the SEC. This means that effective yields on direct placements are being consistently overstated relative to yields on public offerings, perhaps by as much as 10 basis points on the smaller issues and by lesser amounts on the larger issues, *e.g.*, by perhaps 1 or 2 basis points on issues of $10 million and over.

[5] When a fee was paid to an underwriter. Actually, no fee was paid on about half the direct placements and, when no fee was paid, the total cost of flotation is represented by the figure given under "other expenses."

[6] We are disregarding two things: first, the fees paid on direct placements which would raise yields on direct placements relative to yields on public offerings, and second, the difference in other expense which would lower yields on direct placements relative to yields on public offerings. We are saying that these two effects will approximately cancel each other.

Procedure

In order to assess the level of yields on direct placements relative to that on public offerings, time held constant, five steps were taken.

1. Data were collected on all the industrial public offerings and on a 30 per cent random sample of utility public offerings with a face value of $2 million or more, sold from January 1, 1951, through December 31, 1961.[7] The data collected on each issue were: date of offering, yield before deduction of underwriting fees; yield after deduction of underwriting fees; total capitalization (X_2); total interest, five-year average (X_4); size of issue (X_6); type of security (X_5); industrial classification (X_6); EBIT, five-year average (X_{12}); maturity (X_{13}); and the ratio of pro-forma long-term debt to pro-forma total capitalization (X_{15}). The basic data were obtained from Moody's and adjusted as necessary. In the absence of data on years nonrefundable (X_7) and average term (X_3), estimates were made for these two variables.

2. Industrials were separated from utilities, and the observations deposited in the appropriate cells of the matrixes set forth in Charts 6 and 13.[8]

3. Yields net-to-the-issuer were then averaged over each diagonal and quarterly "series" obtained—seven for industrials and eight for utilities.

4. Residuals were obtained quarterly for each series by subtracting yields on public offerings from yields on direct placements. Thus, a positive residual meant a higher yield for the given class and quarter on direct placements and a negative residual, a lower yield.[9] The residuals were then averaged algebraically within each class, over the whole period.

The results of the averaging are given, separately for industrials and utilities, in the first and third columns of Table 64. The residual

[7] About 200 issues of each type, pure debt issues only.

[8] The matrixes were adjusted to give full effect to the fact that some public offerings are sold by very large companies.

[9] Comparisons were possible in less than half the quarters for nearly all series.

TABLE 64

Actual and Computed Yields on Direct Placements
Minus Yields on Public Offerings, by Quality
Class, Eleven-Year Average, 1951–61

| | Average Residuals | | | |
| | Industrials | | Utilities | |
Class	Actual	Computed	Actual	Computed
1	+.45	+.33	––	+.16
2	+.37	+.15	+.63	+.20
3	+.30	+.15	+.44	+.12
4	+.08	–.03	+.29	+.19
5	–.21	–.06	––	+.05
6	––	––	––	+.08

TABLE 65

Actual and Computed Yields on Direct Placements Minus
Yields on Public Offerings, Classes 2, 3, and 4 Only,
Annually, 1951–61

| | Industrials | | Utilities | |
Year	Actual	Computed	Actual	Computed
1951	–.01	–.20	+.34	+.27
1952	+.28	+.22	+.11	+.10
1953	+.33	–.04	+.49	+.04
1954	+.62	+.39	+.29	+.23
1955	+.10	–.15	+.27	+.13
1956	+.06	+.19	+.41	+.24
1957	+.18	+.48	+.46	+.29
1958	+.51	+.43	+.74	+.13
1959	+.80	+.31	+.38	+.13
1960	+.50	+.35	+.23	+.17
1961	+.48	+.02	+.33	+.05

CHART 20

*Industrials and Utilities: Yields on Direct Placements Minus
Yields on Public Offerings, Actual and Computed, Classes 2,
3, and 4 Only, Annually, 1951–61*

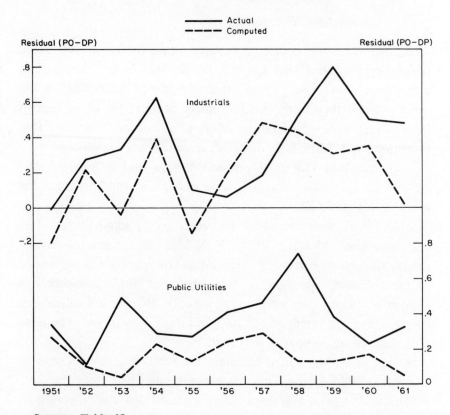

SOURCE: Table 65.

declines steadily from class to class, and for industrials becomes
negative in class 5. (Comparisons were possible for utilities for
only three classes.)

5. The quarterly observations were averaged annually, for
classes 2, 3, and 4 combined (Table 65). These annual averages
are plotted in Chart 20.[10]

[10] Neither quarterly series for the three classes combined nor annual series
for each class separately could be constructed.

The results raised two questions: (1) Why is the residual positive? (2) Why, for industrials and apparently not for utilities, does the residual decline from class to class?

Computed Residuals

Residuals were, of course, compared class by class. But some possibility remained that the public offerings in any given class were, on the average, "better" than the direct placements in the same class. If they were, this fact might account for all or part of the residual in favor of public offerings. In order to be sure that everything was being held constant, residuals were computed.

1. A hundred industrial public offerings and a hundred and twenty utility public offerings were chosen at random from the samples described above.

2. A yield was computed for each by "plugging" the data collected from Moody's on each X into the original quarterly *direct placement* regression equations. This procedure responded to the following question: If this particular public offering had been sold, when it was sold, not as a public offering but rather as a direct placement, *what would the yield on it have been?* The issue was, thus, being compared with itself.[11]

3. Residuals were then obtained for each issue by subtracting the actual yield on the issue (as a public offering) from the computed yield. Again, a positive residual meant that the "theoretical" yield on the issue as a direct placement was higher than the actual yield on the issue when it was sold as a public offering.

4. These computed residuals were deposited in the appropriate class and an average was taken within each class over the whole period. These averages are given by class, separately for industrials and utilities, in the second and fourth columns of Table 64.

The results are interesting. First, holding every thing constant has lowered the level of the residual in every class both for indus-

---

[11] Except to the extent that X_3 and X_7 had been inaccurately estimated.

trials and utilities. Both sets of residuals continue to decline, though not as systematically as before, but the conclusion does appear warranted that the larger better-quality issues do better on the public market, whereas smaller lesser-quality issues appear to do better in the direct placement market. In other words, the public market is willing to pay a premium for the issues of well-known companies and, conversely, tends to exact a penalty, in the form of higher selling costs, on the issues of less well-known or little-known companies. Well-known companies are on the average larger and of better "quality" than little-known companies.

5. Classes 2, 3, and 4 were then combined and annual averages calculated (Chart 20). The cycle in the residual on industrials has virtually disappeared and the upward trend is reduced. The residual on utilities is now fluctuating very slightly around a horizontal line.

The following conclusions are inescapable: (1) The residual "existed" during the period 1951–61 both for industrials and utilities on the issues in fact compared. (2) The residual on both industrials and utilities declines from class to class.

A Suggested Hypothesis

A hypothesis which would explain the above findings follows.

There were, in fact, in the period 1951–61, *two* weighting systems—one for public offerings and one for direct placements. The weighting system for public offerings favored the issues of large well-known companies, whereas the weighting system for direct placements favored the issues of smaller lesser-known companies.

When the characteristics of the issues of large well-known companies are "plugged" into regression equations derived from direct placements, size and reputation of issuer receive less weight than they in fact did receive in the public market. Hence the yield on such an issue tends to be higher as a direct placement than its actual yield as a public offering. But this effect tends to be less in the lower classes simply because, as we go from class to class, size of issuer declines and the issuer itself tends to be less well-known.

This hypothesis would explain the tendency of the residual to decline from class to class. And the residual shows itself to be positive on the whole, over time, simply because the figures in Table 65 were derived from the higher classes, i.e., the classes in which public offerings predominate.[12]

In brief, the foregoing analysis suggests that the direct placement and public markets tend to serve different classes of customers. The direct placement market tends to serve small and medium-sized lesser-known issuers and the public market, the larger better-known issuers.[13]

Last, some large well-known companies directly placed their issues during the period. The foregoing analysis suggests that such issuers could have done better, *in terms of price*, in the public market. Therefore, the residuals given in Table 64, especially for classes 1 through 3, are estimates of the value put by such issuers on the *nonprice* advantages of direct placements.

---

[12] The foregoing hypothesis implies, of course, that if the characteristics of direct placements were "plugged" into a series of regression equations derived from public offerings, the residuals so obtained would favor direct placements during the period in question. Unfortunately, this test was beyond the resources of the present study.

[13] Perhaps the extent to which the markets in fact compete depends on the level of interest rates. When money is tight the direct placement market may compete little if at all for the relatively low-yielding issues of the large well-known companies, and vice versa when money is easy.

Appendix A

SIGNS OF THE COEFFICIENTS

Tables A-1 and A-2 give expected signs and actual signs for each coefficient included in the final reruns. For some coefficients, under the column headed "expected sign," a priori considerations ran in both directions and their net weight was not clear. With respect to b_3 (average term) and b_{13} (maturity), for example, the cross-

TABLE A-1

Industrials: Ten Regression Coefficients, Expected
Sign, Actual Sign Cross Sections, and Actual
Sign "Over-All" Regression

| | | Actual Sign[a] | |
Coefficient	Expected Sign	Cross Sections	Over-All Regression
b_2	−	−	−
b_3	b	−	−
b_{4r}	+	+	+
b_5	+	−	−
b_6	−	−	−
b_7	−	+	+
b_8	b	−	−
b_{12}	−	−	−
b_{13}	b	−	−
b_{15}	b	−	−

[a]See Tables 25 and 26.
[b]The net weight of a priori considerations was unclear.

TABLE A-2

Public Utilities: Ten Regression Coefficients, Expected Sign, Actual Sign Cross Sections, and Actual Sign "Over-All" Regression

		Actual Sign[a]	
			Over-All
	Expected		
Coefficient	Sign	Cross Sections	Regression
b_2	−	−	−
b_3	b	−	−
b_{4r}	+	+	+
b_5	+	+	+
b_6	b	−	−
b_7	−	+	+
b_8	b	−	−
b_{12}	−	−	−
b_{13}	b	+	+
b_{15}	b	−	−

[a]See Tables 43 and 44.
[b]The net weight of a priori considerations was unclear.

section analysis did not hold constant expectations as to the future course of interest rates. Clearly, an expectation that rates would decline could be sufficiently strong to outweigh the greater risk implicit in longer duration. The same kind of consideration applies to the ratio of long-term debt to total capital, given the fact that total interest (i.e., total debt) is being held constant. In other words, given total debt, would we expect lenders to prefer a higher long-term debt ratio or a lower one? So far as utilities are concerned, would we expect that, other things being equal, yields on the issues of electric and telephone companies would be higher or lower than yields on the issues of water and gas distribution companies? Clearly, questions such as these can be answered only by reference to the facts.

Type of Security

Table A-1 indicates that, for industrials, b_5 (type of security) takes the wrong sign. The sign indicates that, other things being equal, yields are lower on debentures than on mortgage bonds. This, of course, is the reverse of the finding which had been expected.

It seems altogether possible that X_5 is really measuring those industry effects not held constant by X_6. X_6 is simply a dummy variable $(0,1)$ which merely distinguishes between producers of durable goods and producers of consumer goods. The b_6 coefficient carried the "right" sign, i.e., yields are lower on the issues of companies which produce consumer goods. But producers of both types of goods vary a good deal among themselves with respect, say, to the stability of earnings. Those who have the better records (or prospects) tend, doubtless, to be more likely to be able to obtain funds on their general credit. In brief, X_5 is probably acting as a proxy for those industry effects not held constant by X_6 as defined. This hypothesis finds some support in the fact that b_5 for utilities carries the right sign (Table A-2); X_6 for utilities holds industry effects much more closely constant than does X_6 for industrials.[1]

It would not have been possible to dummy in the thirty-odd two-digit classes for industrials without reducing degrees of freedom well below zero.

Years Nonrefundable

This coefficient was positive for both industrials and utilities. Neither was very large: a change of one standard deviation in X_7 would be capable of affecting yield by something less than 1 per cent. Nevertheless the sign is clearly positive.

[1] Both b_5,s decline in importance after 1955. Over the period, lenders seem to have cared less about differences in the stability of earnings—perhaps because those differences became smaller (Charts D-1 and D-2).

The simple correlation between yield and X_7 was predominantly negative for industrials and predominantly positive for utilities. This was true for industrials primarily because X_7 was correlated positively with the size and duration variables. The larger companies which, in general, pay less for money, get the longer maturities, and the longer the maturity of an issue, the longer will be the period of nonrefundability. So far as utilities are concerned, however, X_7 tends not to be correlated to any significant extent with any other variable (Table 34) and therefore the sign it carries tends to indicate the direction of its separate effect on yield. In other words, for industrials, when the effects of the other variables with which X_7 is correlated, are "partialled out," X_7 shows itself to be positive.

But the question remains: why does yield vary positively with X_7? The numbers which have been used to quantify X_7 must in fact also be measuring something else which, a priori, would vary positively with yield but which is not included in the regressions. Bargaining strength might be one such variable: if two issues are identical in every respect, but the issuer of the first happens to be in a relatively weaker bargaining position than the issuer of the second, that issuer will pay a relatively higher price for money and may find himself also forced to accept a longer period of nonrefundability. In such a case, the longer period of nonrefundability would merely be a measure of his relative bargaining weakness. This hypothesis may or may not be valid, but we should bear in mind that despite the large number of variables which has here been taken into account, some variables had, perforce, to be omitted. Bargaining strength is one and it is not difficult to think of others on which it would have been equally difficult to collect quantifiable data.

Industrial Class

The sign on this coefficient for utilities means that, other things being equal, yields are somewhat lower on the issues of water and gas distribution companies than on the issues of electric and telephone companies. This finding is not really surprising. The simple correlation between yield and X_6 (Table 34) was positive, but as Table 51 suggests, the issues of water and gas distribution companies are, on the average, of substantially lesser "quality" than the issues of electric and telephone companies. When "quality" is equated as between the two types of issues, yields are found to be somewhat lower on those of water and gas distribution companies.

Average Term and Maturity

When maturity (X_{13}) and size of issue (X_8) are held constant, average term (X_3) measures weighted average amortization, i.e., given two issues of the same size and maturity, average term will be longer on the issue which is amortized later in its life, and vice versa. Table A-3 illustrates this point for two issues of $1 million and five-years maturity. Issue A, which is amortized in equal amounts in each year, has an average term of three years. Issue B, which is not amortized at all in the first three years and is amortized in equal amounts in years four and five, has an average term of four and a half years.[2] With size and maturity held constant, average term is thus an unambiguous measure of duration.

However, with average term and size held constant, maturity has a rather special meaning. If two issues of the same size and average term differ in maturity, their amortization schedules must also differ, and the issue with the longer maturity will tend to be more heavily amortized in the early years of its life. Table A-4 illustrates this point by comparing the amortization schedules of two issues of the same size and average term but of different maturity. Issue A has a maturity of five years and is identical to Issue A in Table A-3. Issue B, however, has a maturity of ten years. In order to equate average term on the two issues, amortiza-

[2] When an issue is not amortized at all during its life but simply paid off in full at maturity, average term and maturity are the same.

TABLE A-3

*Comparison of Average Term of $1 Million Issue of Five-Years
Maturity with Different Amortization Schedules*

Years	Amortization (000 dollars)	Weighted Amortization
	ISSUE "A"	
1	200	200
2	200	400
3	200	600
4	200	800
5	200	1000
Total	1000	3000

$$\text{Average Term} = \frac{3000}{1000} = 3 \text{ Years}$$

Years	Amortization (000 dollars)	Weighted Amortization
	ISSUE "B"	
1	--	--
2	--	--
3	--	--
4	500	2000
5	500	2500
Total	1000	4500

$$\text{Average Term} = \frac{4500}{1000} = 4.5 \text{ Years}$$

tion on the longer issue must be heavier in the earlier, less-heavily
weighted years. In the illustration, 96.5 per cent of Issue B, but
only 80 per cent of Issue A, is amortized in the first four years.
Thus, with average term and size held constant, the coefficient on
maturity is assessing the *net* effect of two opposite influences on
yield—longer final maturity as such and, given that longer life,
heavier amortization in the earlier years of the loan.

The behavior of the coefficients on average term may be summarized as follows:

1. For industrials (Chart D-1), from mid-1953 to the end of 1958 lenders were offering a premium for longer duration—presumably because they expected interest rates to decline. After 1958, this premium disappeared.

2. For utilities (Chart D-2), lenders appeared to prefer longer

TABLE A-4

Comparison of Amortization Schedules of $1 Million Issue of Three-Years Average Term, with Different Maturities

Years	Amortization (000 dollars)	Weighted Amortization
	ISSUE "A"	
1	200	200
2	200	400
3	200	600
4	200	800
5	200	1000
Total	1000	3000

$$\text{Average Term} = \frac{3000}{1000} = 3 \text{ Years}$$

Years	Amortization (000 dollars)	Weighted Amortization
	ISSUE "B"	
1	200	200
2	200	400
3	200	600
4	365	1460
5	--	--
6	--	--
7	--	--
8	--	--
9	--	--
10	35	350
Total	1000	3010

$$\text{Average Term} = \frac{3010}{1000} = 3 \text{ Years}$$

duration through the whole period although this preference weakened noticeably after mid-1958. After mid-1958 none of the coefficients on average term is significant.

The coefficients on maturity are telling us essentially the same tale, namely, that until 1957–58, a borrower who wanted a longer maturity had to take a longer average term also in order to avoid being required to pay a higher yield.

Chart D-1 indicates that until the second quarter of 1958, the coefficient on maturity for industrials was predominantly positive. During this period, it showed eighteen plus and eleven minus signs. But between the second quarter of 1958 and the fourth quarter of 1961, it showed thirteen minus signs and just two plus signs. This sharp change in the behavior of the coefficient between 1958 and 1961 was sufficient to cause the sign to be negative over-all and, on balance, in the cross sections.

The coefficient for utilities showed sixteen plus signs and six minus signs in the cross sections and was positive in the over-all regression. The coefficient was trending strongly downward, however, and was predominantly positive only until the first half of 1957. During this period, eleven of thirteen signs were positive. Thereafter, the coefficient showed five plus and four minus signs— and a weighted average of the last nine coefficients would carry a negative sign.

In short, it appears that "something happened" in 1957–58 which caused b_3 and b_{13} for industrials and b_{13} for utilities to change sign; it also caused b_3 for utilties to weaken substantially.[3]

What happened in 1957–58 which might explain the change in the behavior of these coefficients? The answer is, perhaps, not far to seek. After a trough in mid-1958, interest rates began to rise sharply (e.g. Chart 8) and at the same time, presumably, expectations as to their future course changed drastically.

The results here suggest fairly strongly that we should not

[3] Interestingly enough, the coefficient on maturity for finance company placements showed similar behavior. It was positive for the first two cross sections (1951–54 and 1955–57) but negative in the third (1958–61).

expect the signs on duration variables to be uniformly positive. The signs will tend to be determined in large part by current expectations as to the future course of interest rates.

Long-Term Debt Ratio

The sign on b_{15} simply indicates that, given total debt, lenders prefer companies with less short-term and more long-term debt. This finding can be rationalized readily enough: if a company has relatively less short-term debt, debt service (interest plus amortization) will be less per dollar of total debt, simply because short-term debt must, in general, be fully amortized within the current year.[4] This means that, given total debt, the company with relatively more long-term debt will have more cash available to service its total debt.

When the regressions were run with X_4 omitted, b_{15} carried a plus sign for both industrials and utilities—although, of course, X_4 doubtless acts as a proxy for X_{15} when the latter is omitted.

[4] Either by net cash outlay or by new borrowing.

Appendix B

CHANGING CHARACTERISTICS OF DIRECT PLACEMENTS

This appendix is devoted to tabular description of the behavior of the various significant variables. The data are presented separately for industrials and utilities.

Means and Standard Deviations: Industrials

Table B-6 describes the behavior of the logs of the *geometric* means of X_2, X_3, X_4, X_8, X_{12}, X_{13}, and X_{15}, i.e., of all the significant variables for which logarithms were used. Table B-8 gives the *arithmetic* means for all ten significant variables, including X_5 (type of security), X_6 (industrial class), and X_7 (years non-refundable). Table B-7 gives the standard deviations of the logs of the geometric means and Table B-9, the standard deviations of the arithmetic means. Tables B-1 and B-2 are summary tables which compare the behavior of the means of the significant variables, for industrials, as between the first half (1951–55) and the second half (1956–61) of the period.

These tables tell a very simple story: the size variables, X_2, X_8, and X_{12}, all showed substantial increases between 1951–55 and 1956–61. The geometric mean of X_2, for example, rose from $12.8 million on the average in the earlier period to $24.9 million in the later period. The geometric mean of X_{12} (EBIT) rose from $1.8 million in the earlier period to $2.9 million in the later period. On the other hand, X_4 (which is usually considered to be *the* most important "quality" variable) declined steadily during the period. The geometric mean of X_4 during the years 1951–55 was

TABLE B-1

*Industrials: Average Values for 1951-55 Compared
with Average Values for 1956–61, Geometric
Means of Seven Significant Variables*

Variable	Units	1951–55 (1)	1956–61 (2)	Col. 2 ÷ Col. 1 × 100 (3)
X_2	Million dollars	12.8	24.9	194.5
X_3	Years	9.3	9.8	105.4
X_4	Times	11.8	8.3	70.3
X_8	Million dollars	2.0	2.6	130.0
X_{12}	Years	1.8	2.9	161.1
X_{13}	Years	14.9	15.7	105.4
X_{15}	Dollars of long-term debt per dollar of total capital	.28	.28	100.0

11.8, whereas in 1956–61, it was 8.3 (Table B-1). The variable X_7, years nonrefundable, rose sharply from an average of 4.9 years in 1951–55 to an average of 7.5 years in 1956–61 (Table B-2).[1]

For the most part the other variables, with the exception of X_8 (which rose slightly), showed no material change in one direction or the other. The combination of the increase in EBIT (earnings before interest and taxes) and the decline in times charges earned (which is simply EBIT divided by total pro-forma interest) can be explained by three factors. The first is the sharp rise in interest rates which took place during the period. On the average, for example, rates on industrial direct placements rose from a low of about 3.65 in the first quarter of 1951 to a peak of about 6.00 in the fourth quarter of 1960.

The second is the sharp increase in total capitalization, and the third, the slight increase in the ratio of debt to total capitalization.

In brief, EBIT rose by 60 per cent but interest rates rose by

[1] These figures are *simple* means, i.e., they are not weighted by dollar amount.

TABLE B-2

*Industrials: Average Values for 1951–55 Compared
with Average Values for 1956–61, Arithmetic
Means of Ten Significant Variables*

Variable	Units	1951–55 (1)	1956–61 (2)	Col. 2 ÷ Col. 1 × 100 (3)
X_2	Million dollars	59.2	140.2	236.8
X_3	Years	10.5	10.4	99.0
X_4	Times	15.6	11.6	74.4
X_5	a	1.6	1.6	100.0
X_6	b	0.61	0.63	103.3
X_7	Years	4.9	7.5	153.1
X_8	Million dollars	5.9	7.3	123.7
X_{12}	Million dollars	10.2	19.6	192.2
X_{13}	Years	16.1	16.4	101.9
X_{15}	Dollars of long-term debt per dollar of total capital	0.31	0.32	103.2

aSee note a, Table 29.
bSee note b, Table 29.

about 65 per cent and total debt by something more than 90 per
cent, i.e., by about the same percentage as total capitalization.
Hence, times-charges-earned ratios came down sharply.[2]

CYCLICAL CONFORMITY

No attempt has been made to analyze systematically the cyclical
behavior of the foregoing series. On the basis of the raw data,
four variables show clear signs of cyclical behavior: X_2, X_7, X_8,
and X_{12}. Of these four variables, the behavior of X_7 (years non-

[2] Times charges earned equals EBIT/rD, where r equals average interest rates
and D, total debt outstanding. The numerator of the fraction doubled during the
period but the denominator *quadrupled.*

refundable) is perhaps the most interesting. In the early part of
the period, when rates were relatively low, the series appears to be
conforming negatively. But beginning in 1955, when rates began
to rise sharply, its positive conformity is almost perfect. The
positive conformity in the latter part of the period is what one
would expect: when rates are high, lenders are eager to forestall
call or prevent it altogether. The apparent negative conformity in
the earlier years may merely be random fluctuation around a mean
of four or five years. In any event, there can be no doubt that
the mean value around which the series is fluctuating in 1951–55
is significantly less than the mean value around which it is fluctuating
in 1956–61.

Means and Standard Deviations: Public Utilities

On the whole, public utilities show much the same behavior as
industrials. The size variables showed an increase, X_4, a decrease,

TABLE B-3

*Public Utilities: Average Values for 1951–55 Compared
with Average Values for 1956–61, Geometric
Means of Seven Significant Variables*

Variable	Units	1951–55 (1)	1956–61 (2)	Col. 2 ÷ Col. 1 × 100 (3)
X_2	Million dollars	11.4	16.1	141.2
X_3	Years	19.8	18.8	94.9
X_4	Times	3.1	2.9	93.5
X_8	Million dollars	1.1	1.9	172.7
X_{12}	Years	0.7	2.1	300.0
X_{13}	Years	24.3	24.1	99.1
X_{15}	Dollars of long-term debt per dollar of total capital	.54	.54	100.0

TABLE B-4

Public Utilities: Average Values for 1951—55 Compared
with Average Values for 1956—61, Arithmetic
Means of Ten Significant Variables

Variable	Units	1951—55 (1)	1956—61 (2)	Col. 2 ÷ Col. 1 × 100 (3)
X_2	Million dollars	44.6	77.8	174.4
X_3	Years	21.2	19.9	93.9
X_4	Times	3.6	3.3	91.7
X_5	a	0.3	0.4	133.3
X_6	b	1.47	1.52	103.4
X_7	Years	1.4	5.2	371.4
X_8	Million dollars	4.9	5.7	116.3
X_{12}	Million dollars	2.8	5.1	182.1
X_{13}	Years	25.2	24.7	98.0
X_{15}	Dollars of long-term debt per dollar of total capital	0.56	0.55	98.2

[a]See note a, Table 29.
[b]See note b, Table 29.

and the other variables remained much the same. The changes
from the early part to the latter part of the period for utilities are
summarized in Tables B-3 and B-4. The variables X_2, X_8, and X_{12}
rose sharply (Table B-3) as did X_7 and X_5 (Table B-4); X_4 declined as did X_3. The other variables remained virtually unchanged.

CYCLICAL CONFORMITY

Again, on the basis of the raw data above, X_2, X_8, and X_{12}
(all size variables) show clear signs of cyclical behavior, as does
X_7 and perhaps also X_4 and X_5. Cyclical behavior on the part of
X_5 would mean that in periods of prosperity more utility place-

TABLE B-5

Finance Companies: Average Values for 1951–54 compared
with Average Values for 1955–57 and 1958–61,
Geometric Means of Selected Variables

		1951–54 (1)	1955–57 (2)	1958–61 (3)	Col. 3 ÷ Col. 1 × 100 (4)
X_3	Years	9.2	9.2	9.7	
X_4	Times	2.4	1.8	1.6	66.7
X_5	a	2.8			
X_8	Million dollars	3.5	2.9	2.5	71.4
X_{12}	Million dollars	2.9	2.6	2.3	79.3
X_{13}	Years	12.4	13.1	14.2	114.5
X_{24}	Dollars of net worth per dollar of senior long-term debt	.82	.69	.59	72.0

aSee note a, Table 29.

ments tend to be in the form of debentures, whereas in periods of recession, more tend to be in the form of mortgage bonds.

Principal Variables of Finance Companies

Table B-5 describes the behavior of the principal finance company variables. Average size of issue, earnings, and interest coverage all declined during the period, as did equity-debt ratios. Average term and maturity rose.[3]

[3] Satisfactory quarterly series for finance companies could not be obtained because of the small number of observations.

TABLE B-6

Industrials: Natural Logs of Geometric Means of Seven Significant Variables, Quarterly, 1951–61

Year and Quarter	X_2	X_3	X_4	X_8	X_{12}	X_{13}	X_{15}
1951							
1	9.5169	2.1967	2.7083	7.8253	7.6607	2.6584	-1.3053
2	9.6034	2.1658	2.6029	7.7477	7.6545	2.6424	-1.2588
3	8.7762	2.1399	2.5411	7.1219	6.8190	2.6053	-1.2356
4	9.9401	2.4058	2.5195	8.4086	8.0337	2.8529	-1.1946
1952							
1	9.7485	2.2968	2.4503	7.8658	7.8062	2.7691	-1.1570
2	9.6814	2.3164	2.7734	7.7424	7.8499	2.7737	-1.3818
3	9.1434	2.0980	2.5544	7.2776	7.1794	2.6289	-1.3757
4	9.7683	2.2749	2.4229	7.8786	7.7093	2.7413	-1.0655
1953							
1	9.2634	2.2080	2.2308	7.4513	7.2038	2.6905	-1.2252
2	9.4265	2.1438	2.4792	7.5898	7.3971	2.6163	-1.3889
3	8.9839	2.1134	2.5494	7.0473	7.0462	2.6849	-1.3866
4	9.6687	2.3114	2.4854	7.5769	7.7538	2.7085	-1.3245
1954							
1	9.3666	2.2462	2.4684	7.5530	7.4532	2.7357	-1.3340
2	9.2930	2.1476	2.4723	7.3980	7.3000	2.6381	-1.3591
3	9.5762	2.3062	2.3155	7.4310	7.5068	2.7445	-1.1904
4	9.9393	2.2877	2.4726	7.8252	7.8720	2.7832	-1.3336
1955							
1	8.9012	2.2129	2.3525	7.0710	6.9989	2.6837	-1.1822
2	9.5868	2.3149	2.3659	7.6759	7.5527	2.8059	-1.2403
3	9.2754	2.1621	2.4088	7.4792	7.2901	2.6537	-1.2273
4	9.2536	2.2185	2.0533	7.5069	7.1602	2.6478	-1.1145
1956							
1	9.4491	2.2001	2.0332	7.6660	7.3309	2.6922	-1.0605
2	9.8157	2.2285	2.3136	7.8163	7.6628	2.6749	-1.2652
3	10.4485	2.3265	2.4039	8.0168	8.3865	2.7368	-1.3251
4	10.3435	2.3569	1.9969	8.3149	8.0879	2.8145	-1.1556
1957							
1	9.9961	2.2692	2.1657	7.8295	7.9495	2.7544	-1.2011
2	10.5580	2.3824	2.3498	8.0730	8.5130	2.8092	-1.4381
3	10.3081	2.4723	2.0916	8.2390	8.1217	2.8693	-1.2625
4	10.5903	2.4923	2.1958	8.5394	8.5089	2.9183	-1.3585
1958							
1	10.0002	2.3117	2.1640	8.0348	7.8686	2.7995	-1.3738
2	10.5803	2.2913	2.4517	7.6903	8.5187	2.7932	-1.4930
3	10.0437	2.3565	2.0131	8.1641	7.8487	2.8359	-1.2222
4	10.4073	2.2949	2.3078	7.8378	8.1781	2.8217	-1.3370
1959							
1	10.3479	2.2648	2.7438	7.3461	8.3754	2.7621	-1.7344
2	10.2928	2.2245	2.1070	7.7104	8.0936	2.7171	-1.2855
3	10.7433	2.4120	2.0855	7.9593	8.5041	2.8449	-1.4054
4	9.8227	2.1373	2.0957	7.5922	7.5873	2.6460	-1.4815
1960							
1	10.9988	2.3121	1.7460	8.3628	8.7121	2.6691	-1.0726
2	10.1327	2.2756	1.8832	7.9297	7.8300	2.7958	-1.3093
3	10.1417	2.2575	2.1305	7.8643	7.9234	2.7310	-1.3474
4	9.5236	2.2506	1.8376	7.3822	7.2454	2.7377	-1.2075
1961							
1	9.7804	2.2358	1.8484	7.7267	7.6595	2.6775	-1.0731
2	9.9323	2.1856	1.9712	7.8942	7.6977	2.6930	-1.2590
3	9.6318	2.2400	1.9070	7.7206	7.4837	2.7064	-1.1421
4	9.8494	2.2803	2.3564	7.7205	7.9559	2.7918	-1.3530

TABLE B-7

*Industrials: Standard Deviations of Natural Logs of Geometric
Means of Seven Significant Variables, Quarterly, 1951–61*

Year and Quarter	X_2	X_3	X_4	X_8	X_{12}	X_{13}	X_{15}
1951							
1	1.6352	0.3706	0.6986	1.5486	1.6947	0.3291	0.4503
2	1.4223	0.3383	0.7448	1.2890	1.3907	0.2854	0.3594
3	1.5172	0.5181	0.5736	1.4161	1.6439	0.4122	0.3823
4	2.1809	0.6216	0.5530	2.2410	1.9940	0.4859	0.2391
1952							
1	1.4351	0.4762	0.6646	1.4583	1.4200	0.3900	0.3118
2	1.5805	0.4590	0.4105	1.5643	1.6055	0.3559	0.5505
3	1.5898	0.4038	0.6144	1.3574	1.6579	0.4067	0.3758
4	1.6516	0.3905	0.8341	1.3326	1.8236	0.3065	0.4073
1953							
1	1.2222	0.3761	0.6770	0.9965	1.3994	0.2779	0.3762
2	1.6270	0.4029	0.5360	1.4833	1.7713	0.3228	0.3559
3	1.4632	0.2382	0.5159	0.8405	1.5225	0.2337	0.3047
4	1.5565	0.2760	0.7782	1.3448	1.5159	0.2079	0.6851
1954							
1	1.8429	0.5135	0.8180	1.6627	1.8826	0.4092	0.5363
2	1.3277	0.3577	0.7938	1.0646	1.5024	0.3081	0.4998
3	2.1532	0.7438	0.8394	1.6401	2.3476	0.6315	0.4013
4	1.7575	0.3483	0.8828	1.5807	1.7664	0.2830	0.5565
1955							
1	1.2912	0.3719	0.7782	1.0450	1.4054	0.3694	0.4190
2	1.9998	0.4162	0.7720	1.3801	2.2027	0.3420	0.3390
3	1.2858	0.3702	0.7071	1.2543	1.3339	0.3169	0.3370
4	1.5856	0.3684	0.7690	1.3147	1.4818	0.3185	0.4738
1956							
1	1.6156	0.4116	0.6757	1.3557	1.5849	0.3535	0.4496
2	1.7723	0.3503	0.7814	1.3466	1.6860	0.3271	0.5120
3	1.9619	0.3848	1.0789	1.4420	2.1238	0.2549	0.8920
4	1.8991	0.2970	0.6327	1.5387	1.8688	0.2265	0.4078
1957							
1	1.4774	0.3455	0.5469	1.4124	1.4380	0.3032	0.3344
2	2.0113	0.3494	1.0103	1.5266	1.9427	0.3114	0.7623
3	1.0449	0.2205	0.5718	1.4537	1.0768	0.2373	0.4473
4	1.5511	0.2386	0.9351	1.5810	1.7545	0.2653	0.5868
1958							
1	1.2569	0.2353	0.8382	1.1090	1.2074	0.2043	0.6751
2	1.9323	0.3518	1.2119	1.5823	1.9735	0.3679	1.0123
3	1.9244	0.2364	0.8278	1.2424	2.0543	0.1991	0.4546
4	1.8510	0.2752	0.9612	1.3355	1.9559	0.2646	0.4187
1959							
1	1.7137	0.2506	1.6330	1.3169	1.6436	0.2703	1.5589
2	2.0942	0.3382	0.6828	1.3454	2.2255	0.3367	0.4521
3	1.7762	0.3813	0.8504	1.3153	1.8327	0.3570	0.5778
4	1.2816	0.3326	0.7612	1.2411	1.2895	0.3289	0.6092
1960							
1	2.0443	0.3212	0.6677	1.6947	2.1907	0.3038	0.3951
2	1.9254	0.3004	0.5819	1.4456	1.8986	0.2646	0.4462
3	1.6176	0.2581	1.0240	1.4019	1.6371	0.2301	0.8361
4	2.2125	0.3198	0.8880	1.4937	2.2845	0.3365	0.5802
1961							
1	1.7553	0.3407	0.5050	1.4703	1.6739	0.3868	0.3282
2	1.8074	0.4108	0.6941	1.3714	1.8447	0.4353	0.3982
3	1.7609	0.3331	0.7293	1.1995	1.8656	0.3421	0.3458
4	1.6561	0.2654	0.9831	1.1809	1.6061	0.2138	0.6246

Appendix B

TABLE B-8

Industrials: Arithmetic Means of Ten Significant Variables,
Quarterly, 1951–61

Year and Quarter	X_2	X_3	X_4	X_5	X_6	X_7	X_8	X_{12}	X_{13}	X_{15}
1951										
1	46.3	9.6	19.6	1.6	0.72	3.7	8.8	7.2	15.0	0.30
2	44.0	9.2	18.9	1.8	0.54	5.2	6.7	6.1	14.6	0.30
3	17.8	10.0	15.2	1.5	0.40	5.2	3.0	3.1	15.0	0.31
4	166.7	14.6	14.4	1.8	0.45	6.6	47.7	20.9	20.2	0.31
1952										
1	43.4	12.0	13.8	1.5	0.55	8.2	7.8	6.0	17.8	0.33
2	48.5	11.3	17.4	1.8	0.78	5.5	7.6	7.3	17.1	0.32
3	55.6	8.8	15.4	1.4	0.63	2.9	5.7	7.8	14.8	0.27
4	50.0	10.5	16.4	1.5	0.62	6.2	5.9	7.2	16.2	0.38
1953										
1	23.6	9.8	11.4	1.8	0.62	3.8	2.8	3.7	15.3	0.31
2	57.9	9.2	13.7	1.7	0.47	2.5	6.6	7.6	14.3	0.27
3	40.6	8.5	14.4	1.3	0.63	2.4	1.6	4.4	15.1	0.26
4	49.2	10.5	15.7	1.6	0.54	5.6	4.6	6.7	15.3	0.31
1954										
1	66.5	11.8	17.8	1.4	0.69	6.1	11.8	11.0	17.4	0.29
2	28.9	9.1	17.4	1.6	0.62	3.7	3.0	4.8	14.6	0.28
3	205.3	15.7	16.3	1.5	0.62	9.5	8.0	67.8	20.5	0.33
4	86.7	10.4	17.6	1.6	0.72	4.6	7.7	11.6	16.8	0.29
1955										
1	19.2	9.8	14.9	1.4	0.57	2.5	2.0	3.4	15.6	0.33
2	110.2	11.1	13.9	1.6	0.69	5.4	6.4	22.0	17.6	0.31
3	21.3	9.2	14.1	1.6	0.59	3.2	3.7	3.3	14.9	0.31
4	32.7	9.8	10.4	1.5	0.62	4.4	4.0	3.7	14.8	0.37
1956										
1	49.8	9.8	9.3	1.8	0.62	2.4	6.2	5.6	15.7	0.38
2	121.9	9.8	13.5	1.8	0.44	5.6	7.5	13.5	15.2	0.32
3	203.7	11.1	60.4	1.6	0.65	8.0	11.7	39.2	15.9	0.33
4	154.8	11.0	8.7	1.4	0.65	7.4	12.5	16.9	17.1	0.34
1957										
1	84.9	10.3	10.1	1.7	0.59	9.0	8.4	10.9	16.5	0.32
2	198.8	11.5	20.4	1.3	0.63	11.7	8.8	23.2	17.4	0.29
3	46.4	12.1	9.4	2.0	0.58	10.0	8.0	5.2	18.1	0.31
4	95.0	12.4	14.7	1.7	0.67	10.3	11.9	14.5	19.1	0.29
1958										
1	52.6	10.4	11.9	1.6	0.70	7.4	5.0	5.4	16.8	0.30
2	172.3	10.4	78.4	1.5	0.53	5.7	6.2	23.3	17.3	0.27
3	236.3	10.9	10.4	1.5	0.57	7.9	8.2	36.5	17.4	0.33
4	203.1	10.3	20.1	1.5	0.61	6.2	6.1	24.5	17.4	0.29
1959										
1	108.0	9.9	160.4	1.3	0.73	8.0	2.7	14.6	16.4	0.29
2	213.1	9.8	9.9	0.9	0.54	5.2	5.4	27.8	16.0	0.30
3	193.5	11.8	11.5	1.2	0.62	7.7	6.5	28.8	18.1	0.28
4	36.6	8.9	11.0	1.8	0.62	9.2	3.9	4.1	14.8	0.26
1960										
1	225.3	10.6	7.4	1.6	0.79	7.6	13.0	26.3	15.1	0.36
2	139.9	10.2	7.7	1.4	0.68	9.0	6.9	14.8	16.9	0.30
3	85.0	9.9	18.9	1.5	0.75	8.7	6.9	10.5	15.8	0.32
4	179.8	10.0	9.6	1.6	0.57	7.1	4.8	25.4	16.3	0.34
1961										
1	65.1	9.8	7.2	1.4	0.69	6.2	5.9	6.3	15.4	0.36
2	116.2	9.6	9.0	1.6	0.69	7.7	7.2	16.3	15.9	0.31
3	148.0	9.9	9.1	1.8	0.65	7.4	4.1	29.6	15.8	0.34
4	105.5	10.1	21.3	1.8	0.78	7.2	3.9	24.3	16.7	0.29

TABLE B-9

Industrials: Standard Deviations of Arithmetic Means,
Ten Significant Variables, Quarterly, 1951—61

Year and Quarter	X_2	X_3	X_4	X_5	X_6	X_7	X_8	X_{12}	X_{13}	X_{15}
1951										
1	81.5	3.6	18.3	0.8	0.45	6.6	18.7	11.3	4.6	0.12
2	83.5	3.4	24.9	0.6	0.50	7.1	14.7	12.3	4.2	0.11
3	26.2	7.7	12.1	0.9	0.50	7.7	4.0	5.0	8.8	0.14
4	322.0	17.6	7.8	0.6	0.51	8.9	99.5	42.6	16.7	0.07
1952										
1	76.7	14.3	7.5	0.8	0.50	16.8	18.1	10.2	13.6	0.12
2	73.8	5.6	7.8	0.6	0.42	7.8	14.4	10.0	6.3	0.40
3	177.9	3.4	11.4	0.9	0.49	6.9	19.0	23.2	5.1	0.08
4	68.3	4.4	21.1	0.9	0.50	8.7	9.0	10.8	4.7	0.19
1953										
1	41.6	4.3	7.2	0.7	0.50	7.4	3.3	7.7	4.4	0.10
2	150.6	3.8	7.3	0.7	0.51	5.1	13.5	17.1	4.0	0.10
3	133.6	2.2	7.2	1.0	0.50	5.4	1.4	11.5	3.7	0.08
4	86.1	3.0	12.7	0.9	0.51	6.4	7.8	11.2	3.2	0.16
1954										
1	175.8	15.4	27.9	1.0	0.47	17.0	41.8	35.8	14.5	0.13
2	58.0	3.4	24.9	0.8	0.49	6.1	4.1	9.5	4.3	0.11
3	657.3	24.9	28.9	0.9	0.50	24.4	21.2	297.0	23.5	0.12
4	177.3	3.6	19.8	0.8	0.45	6.9	12.0	21.9	4.4	0.12
1955										
1	33.5	3.8	16.5	0.9	0.50	5.8	2.5	7.1	5.7	0.13
2	263.6	5.6	10.3	0.8	0.47	9.0	13.1	62.3	6.7	0.10
3	26.1	3.1	12.6	0.8	0.50	5.1	5.6	4.9	4.3	0.10
4	53.6	3.6	10.1	0.9	0.49	6.2	5.4	5.9	4.3	0.19
1956										
1	104.3	4.0	5.9	0.6	0.49	4.6	13.0	11.3	5.6	0.17
2	319.8	3.3	11.4	0.7	0.50	6.3	20.2	47.2	4.8	0.15
3	445.8	4.8	327.8	0.9	0.48	7.2	36.9	102.4	4.1	0.20
4	329.4	3.2	4.5	1.0	0.48	6.7	20.9	46.7	3.9	0.16
1957										
1	206.6	4.4	5.9	0.8	0.50	6.8	21.2	33.0	5.9	0.12
2	398.6	3.8	40.1	0.9	0.49	6.9	13.0	53.4	5.6	0.14
3	44.9	2.8	5.5	0.0	0.51	7.8	8.7	5.6	4.3	0.11
4	134.6	3.0	21.4	0.9	0.49	5.7	12.8	21.0	5.2	0.12
1958										
1	115.4	2.3	12.1	0.8	0.47	5.9	4.6	9.4	3.2	0.15
2	325.6	3.0	362.3	0.8	0.51	6.0	8.7	46.2	5.4	0.09
3	646.8	2.9	9.4	0.8	0.50	7.4	14.6	104.2	3.9	0.17
4	579.8	3.0	45.6	0.8	0.50	6.9	10.6	74.9	4.8	0.12
1959										
1	193.3	2.6	542.2	1.0	0.46	8.2	2.1	26.2	4.7	0.18
2	617.4	3.3	5.7	1.0	0.51	5.6	8.9	81.3	5.6	0.13
3	453.8	3.8	11.7	1.0	0.49	8.0	12.0	89.7	5.0	0.12
4	46.9	2.5	10.5	0.5	0.50	6.9	4.6	6.2	4.3	0.12
1960										
1	377.9	3.4	6.9	0.9	0.43	5.2	18.1	46.1	4.8	0.12
2	292.9	2.9	4.9	0.9	0.48	6.4	9.6	33.9	4.4	0.13
3	172.5	2.6	48.8	0.9	0.44	6.6	11.8	21.7	3.8	0.16
4	540.9	3.1	12.3	0.7	0.50	4.7	8.1	90.6	5.8	0.15
1961										
1	127.3	3.0	3.6	0.9	0.47	5.7	9.2	10.2	4.8	0.11
2	296.2	3.5	6.4	0.8	0.47	5.5	11.9	60.8	5.4	0.13
3	611.9	3.4	8.7	0.7	0.49	6.0	5.2	133.9	5.0	0.10
4	334.9	2.8	43.7	0.7	0.43	6.8	3.7	8.9	3.6	0.11

TABLE B-10

*Public Utilities: Natural Logs of Geometric Means of
Seven Significant Variables, Quarterly, 1951–61*

Year and Quarter	X_2	X_3	X_4	X_8	X_{12}	X_{13}	X_{14}
1951							
1	8.7016	2.9801	0.7294	6.8834	5.4254	3.1798	-0.5737
2	9.4971	3.0322	1.3634	7.3893	6.6983	3.1227	-0.8238
3	8.8168	2.9823	1.0545	6.9440	5.9716	3.2107	-0.5790
4	9.4010	3.1031	1.2054	7.2040	6.0964	3.2804	-0.5733
1952							
1	10.0682	3.1094	1.2574	7.6928	7.3325	3.2671	-0.5919
2	9.5442	2.9514	0.9756	7.2851	6.6436	3.1810	-0.5384
3	9.1975	2.8907	1.3295	6.7880	6.6232	3.1079	-0.6154
4	9.6651	2.9894	1.4944	7.4072	6.9449	3.1867	-0.8392
1953							
1	9.9604	2.7378	1.0516	8.2027	7.1478	2.9793	-0.6026
2	10.5684	3.1975	1.1066	8.2338	7.7766	3.3202	-0.5369
3	9.9100	3.1236	1.0797	7.7681	7.1012	3.2598	-0.6233
4	9.3781	2.9137	1.0994	7.2303	6.5622	3.1927	-0.5972
1954							
1	9.6003	3.0850	1.2012	7.9636	6.9503	3.2770	-0.5430
2	9.1093	2.9674	1.1492	6.9398	6.3897	3.1909	-0.5548
3	9.4794	3.0481	1.1058	7.1328	6.6402	3.2513	-0.6091
4	9.1951	2.9454	0.8905	7.1963	6.2394	3.1570	-0.5821
1955							
1	9.4002	3.0325	1.2029	7.4841	6.6567	3.2321	-0.6494
2	8.7640	2.9888	1.2572	6.8870	6.0521	3.1811	-0.6392
3	8.5326	2.9156	0.9960	6.6032	5.6750	3.1553	-0.5185
4	8.5639	2.7990	1.1162	6.6113	5.8281	3.1142	-0.6223
1956							
1	9.4752	2.7900	1.2032	7.4511	6.8206	3.1368	-0.5869
2	9.3893	3.0989	1.0783	7.2977	6.6266	3.2234	-0.6236
3	9.2262	2.9913	0.9443	7.2119	6.3729	3.2504	-0.5708
4	9.3749	2.8754	1.0242	7.3580	6.7228	3.0925	-0.5868
1957							
1	9.7346	2.9631	0.9818	7.5105	6.9607	3.1499	-0.6160
2	9.6386	3.0301	1.1229	7.3637	6.9188	3.2606	-0.6489
3	10.0513	2.9253	1.0835	7.8067	7.3531	3.1829	-0.5787
4	9.9571	3.1164	1.1961	7.8063	7.3285	3.2955	-0.6405
1958							
1	10.0526	2.9560	1.2884	7.7654	7.5160	3.1763	-0.6416
2	9.7230	2.9454	1.1865	7.6372	7.1350	3.1896	-0.6233
3	8.7943	2.8725	1.1658	6.8031	6.2292	3.1371	-0.6372
4	9.4432	2.9215	1.0455	7.2390	6.7694	3.2024	-0.6304
1959							
1	10.1422	3.0905	1.1860	7.8395	7.5380	3.2576	-0.6535
2	10.5955	3.9066	0.9794	8.1372	7.8763	3.2142	-0.5913
3	9.6380	2.8616	0.7602	7.7743	6.8076	3.1262	-0.6065
4	9.8025	3.1603	0.7990	7.6402	6.9273	3.3231	-0.5610
1960							
1	10.2166	2.8604	1.1106	7.8199	7.6733	3.1833	-0.5659
2	9.7988	2.9171	1.0583	7.8518	7.1762	3.1618	-0.6435
3	8.9320	2.9023	0.8972	6.9441	6.2512	3.1307	-0.5920
4	9.7850	2.9434	0.8176	7.5314	6.8629	3.2506	-0.6618
1961							
1	9.4038	2.8607	1.1244	7.2570	6.8323	3.1476	-0.5892
2	9.2725	2.8319	1.1687	7.0302	6.7496	3.1440	-0.6467
3	10.5678	3.0436	0.9856	8.3104	7.8809	3.2446	-0.6343
4	10.2593	2.9783	1.1293	8.1115	7.6486	3.1554	-0.6879

TABLE B-11

Public Utilities: Standard Deviations of Natural Logs of Geometric Means of Seven Significant Variables, Quarterly, 1951–61

Year and Quarter	X_2	X_3	X_4	X_8	X_{12}	X_{13}	X_{14}
1951							
1	1.2635	0.5517	0.4412	1.0980	1.3973	0.3625	0.4422
2	1.5553	0.4947	0.4666	1.3691	1.5942	0.4955	0.3177
3	1.7352	0.3179	0.5345	1.4382	1.8861	0.1837	0.2149
4	1.5608	0.3305	0.4098	1.4149	1.6248	0.2599	0.1135
1952							
1	0.9377	0.3569	0.3656	1.0360	1.0953	0.2334	0.1143
2	1.5329	0.3934	0.3941	1.4589	1.5288	0.2084	0.1532
3	1.6321	0.4394	0.4455	1.1972	1.5319	0.3174	0.2937
4	1.8579	0.4513	0.7497	1.6396	1.8907	0.3233	0.4420
1953							
1	1.9685	0.4844	0.4321	1.8311	1.9214	0.4402	0.2033
2	1.2199	0.2392	0.5604	1.5062	1.5959	0.0961	0.1597
3	1.4835	0.3305	0.4758	1.4852	1.5523	0.2152	0.2480
4	1.2802	0.2625	0.6764	1.1377	1.5867	0.1876	0.1779
1954							
1	1.5212	0.3126	0.3862	1.3850	1.6334	0.1487	0.1749
2	1.1311	0.3655	0.4797	1.0061	1.2895	0.2098	0.1840
3	2.1256	0.3462	0.4960	1.6005	2.3160	0.2375	0.1038
4	1.3350	0.5942	0.5294	1.3925	1.6076	0.4912	0.1626
1955							
1	2.1969	0.3618	0.5839	1.7760	2.3080	0.2109	0.2899
2	1.5877	0.2872	0.5917	1.1836	1.6882	0.1961	0.2398
3	1.7896	0.3056	0.4424	1.6878	1.9508	0.1612	0.2275
4	1.1717	0.4335	0.5693	0.7729	1.4409	0.3673	0.1633
1956							
1	1.5746	0.3520	0.4768	1.5639	1.6019	0.1523	0.2348
2	1.8675	0.2436	0.5340	1.4388	1.9111	0.1752	0.1623
3	1.0257	0.2669	0.5971	0.9580	1.2636	0.1036	0.1641
4	1.6362	0.4013	0.5550	1.3505	1.7627	0.3127	0.2678
1957							
1	1.5277	0.4206	0.6946	1.3602	1.7731	0.2661	0.2044
2	1.3771	0.2261	0.6047	1.0526	1.5240	0.1284	0.2107
3	1.8066	0.3976	0.5490	1.7612	1.8552	0.2499	0.1665
4	1.4525	0.2930	0.3415	1.2264	1.4635	0.1976	0.1199
1958							
1	1.3346	0.2831	0.5582	1.2956	1.4626	0.1355	0.1789
2	1.9782	0.3385	0.5413	1.7804	1.8359	0.2088	0.1982
3	1.4750	0.3568	0.6225	1.3680	1.5438	0.1652	0.2972
4	1.6048	0.2824	0.4414	1.3547	1.7630	0.1923	0.1800
1959							
1	1.1922	0.2963	0.3679	1.1152	1.1778	0.2315	0.2402
2	2.3269	0.3708	0.4398	1.9402	2.2348	0.2867	0.1421
3	1.5068	0.3110	0.6188	1.6461	1.7233	0.2527	0.1628
4	1.5999	0.2825	0.5743	1.1211	1.7687	0.0867	0.1231
1960							
1	1.6427	0.3285	0.3671	1.3262	1.5540	0.1860	0.1599
2	1.3857	0.2916	0.7153	1.2354	1.4844	0.1892	0.2276
3	2.0896	0.2985	0.4181	1.8899	2.2711	0.1570	0.1685
4	1.3980	0.3708	0.7816	1.0716	1.7913	0.1348	0.2272
1961							
1	1.4295	0.4263	0.3651	1.1964	1.4738	0.2915	0.1731
2	1.7700	0.4012	0.4664	1.1921	1.7949	0.2665	0.1587
3	2.0464	0.2725	0.3973	1.8341	2.0830	0.1501	0.1180
4	1.3812	0.4351	0.4463	1.2125	1.5721	0.4048	0.1928

TABLE B-12

*Public Utilities: Arithmetic Means of Ten Significant
Variables, Quarterly, 1951–61*

Year and Quarter	X_2	X_3	X_4	X_5	X_6	X_7	X_8	X_{12}	X_{13}	X_{15}
1951										
1	10.6	22.0	2.3	0.2	1.82	0.8	1.5	0.5	25.3	0.60
2	27.3	22.6	4.3	0.4	1.30	0.7	3.4	1.7	24.6	0.46
3	31.4	20.6	3.2	0.0	1.53	0.6	3.0	2.1	25.2	0.57
4	37.0	23.3	3.6	0.2	1.31	2.6	3.5	2.5	27.4	0.57
1952										
1	36.1	23.5	3.7	0.2	1.18	0.3	3.2	2.7	26.8	0.56
2	44.1	20.5	2.9	0.3	1.38	0.0	6.6	2.1	24.5	0.59
3	40.3	19.6	4.1	0.5	1.46	0.7	1.7	2.9	23.4	0.56
4	69.5	21.5	6.3	0.4	1.28	1.4	5.6	4.2	25.3	0.46
1953										
1	103.4	17.2	3.1	0.5	1.76	1.5	18.6	5.5	21.3	0.56
2	72.6	25.1	3.4	0.2	1.33	2.2	8.3	6.1	27.8	0.59
3	56.9	23.8	3.3	0.4	1.48	3.6	6.2	3.2	26.6	0.55
4	23.3	19.0	3.8	0.1	1.57	0.9	2.5	1.8	24.7	0.56
1954										
1	43.4	22.8	3.6	0.1	1.47	4.4	9.6	3.7	26.8	0.59
2	15.7	20.6	3.5	0.4	1.40	0.3	1.6	1.3	24.8	0.58
3	73.2	22.2	3.3	0.1	1.60	2.5	3.1	4.6	26.5	0.55
4	20.5	21.2	2.7	0.1	1.41	1.3	2.9	1.4	25.2	0.57
1955										
1	107.3	22.0	3.8	0.3	1.33	0.0	9.0	5.4	25.8	0.54
2	18.3	20.6	4.1	0.8	1.50	0.3	1.8	1.2	24.5	0.54
3	39.2	19.3	3.0	0.4	1.62	1.2	3.6	3.1	23.8	0.61
4	9.2	17.7	3.6	0.3	1.53	0.9	1.0	0.8	23.6	0.54
1956										
1	36.6	17.3	3.7	0.6	1.79	1.9	5.4	3.5	23.3	0.57
2	79.2	22.8	3.3	0.2	1.55	3.1	4.4	4.0	25.5	0.54
3	16.3	20.6	3.0	0.1	1.36	2.9	2.1	1.1	25.9	0.57
4	57.2	19.0	3.1	0.5	1.75	6.0	4.0	5.6	23.0	0.57
1957										
1	86.6	20.9	3.2	0.5	1.55	5.6	4.4	4.9	24.1	0.55
2	32.1	21.2	3.8	0.4	1.32	5.8	2.7	2.3	26.3	0.53
3	111.4	19.9	3.3	0.5	1.33	8.2	9.8	6.4	24.8	0.57
4	40.9	23.4	3.5	0.3	1.23	8.0	4.4	3.0	27.5	0.53
1958										
1	83.4	19.9	4.2	0.3	1.28	5.1	6.1	6.4	24.2	0.53
2	126.1	20.1	3.8	0.5	1.54	4.6	9.4	6.3	24.8	0.54
3	23.2	18.7	3.9	0.3	1.68	4.0	3.0	2.2	23.3	0.55
4	37.3	19.2	3.1	0.4	1.56	4.9	2.8	2.9	25.0	0.54
1959										
1	46.5	22.8	3.5	0.3	1.27	4.5	4.3	3.4	26.5	0.53
2	301.7	19.5	2.9	0.4	1.55	3.2	15.5	16.3	26.0	0.56
3	40.1	18.3	2.5	0.4	1.87	7.7	7.9	2.8	23.4	0.55
4	50.2	24.3	2.5	0.3	1.33	5.3	3.5	3.9	27.8	0.57
1960										
1	140.2	18.4	3.2	0.1	1.67	4.7	7.2	8.0	24.5	0.58
2	52.6	19.2	3.6	0.7	1.47	6.0	5.4	3.9	24.0	0.54
3	36.9	19.0	2.6	0.7	1.61	5.8	3.6	3.5	23.2	0.56
4	33.5	20.0	2.8	0.3	1.50	2.8	3.0	2.3	26.0	0.53
1961										
1	30.0	18.8	3.3	0.3	1.52	4.7	2.7	2.4	24.1	0.56
2	84.3	18.2	3.6	0.4	1.48	5.6	3.5	5.4	23.9	0.53
3	159.3	21.7	2.9	0.5	1.45	4.8	11.3	12.8	25.9	0.53
4	60.9	21.1	3.4	0.3	1.86	4.1	7.3	5.2	24.9	0.51

TABLE B-13

Public Utilities: Standard Deviations of Arithmetic Means of Ten Significant Variables, Quarterly, 1951–61

Year and Quarter	X_2	X_3	X_4	X_5	X_6	X_7	X_8	X_{12}	X_{13}	X_{15}
1951										
1	10.7	8.9	1.1	0.6	0.87	1.5	1.1	0.5	7.0	0.17
2	27.1	8.0	1.7	0.8	0.48	1.6	4.4	1.8	7.7	0.13
3	64.7	5.6	1.5	0.0	0.62	1.5	5.5	4.1	4.3	0.13
4	56.5	6.3	1.3	0.7	0.48	7.6	5.4	3.9	6.4	0.06
1952										
1	41.5	6.5	1.2	0.6	0.40	0.6	2.8	3.5	5.3	0.06
2	87.8	7.3	1.3	0.8	0.65	0.0	17.7	3.2	4.8	0.09
3	97.6	8.1	1.9	0.9	0.52	1.7	2.1	7.4	6.9	0.14
4	132.2	7.5	7.5	0.9	0.46	2.1	9.6	6.8	6.8	0.14
1953										
1	164.5	7.8	1.3	0.9	0.75	2.8	34.6	8.4	7.7	0.11
2	80.7	5.5	1.7	0.7	0.50	2.6	8.6	7.9	2.6	0.09
3	117.1	6.6	1.8	0.8	0.59	2.5	9.5	5.5	4.9	0.12
4	25.6	4.8	3.4	0.3	0.51	1.3	2.6	2.0	4.0	0.09
1954										
1	67.1	6.6	1.5	0.5	0.62	9.6	23.1	6.4	3.8	0.10
2	18.0	6.9	1.3	0.8	0.51	0.5	1.8	2.0	5.0	0.12
3	152.2	6.9	1.4	0.5	0.74	7.7	3.9	8.7	5.7	0.06
4	28.0	7.2	1.2	0.4	0.50	3.3	3.6	2.2	6.5	0.10
1955										
1	328.8	7.2	1.8	0.8	0.59	0.0	22.7	14.6	4.9	0.12
2	27.4	5.8	2.4	1.1	0.51	1.1	2.2	1.8	4.6	0.11
3	114.2	5.7	1.3	0.8	0.62	5.0	7.2	9.4	3.9	0.13
4	11.4	6.0	2.3	0.7	0.51	1.2	1.1	1.4	5.7	0.09
1956										
1	57.9	6.4	1.9	0.9	0.58	2.4	9.6	7.5	3.7	0.13
2	212.7	5.3	1.3	0.6	0.69	3.8	8.7	9.8	4.3	0.09
3	19.0	5.1	1.5	0.5	0.50	2.8	2.5	1.2	2.7	0.09
4	161.2	6.7	1.4	0.9	0.61	4.4	6.6	17.1	6.0	0.13
1957										
1	296.1	7.5	1.7	1.0	0.60	3.4	7.7	14.3	5.9	0.11
2	36.9	4.6	3.2	0.8	0.48	3.3	3.5	2.7	3.2	0.11
3	234.2	6.6	1.4	0.9	0.56	3.4	18.2	12.0	5.1	0.10
4	40.0	6.1	1.1	0.7	0.43	3.0	4.3	3.0	4.8	0.06
1958										
1	233.4	5.2	2.3	0.8	0.46	2.4	11.9	15.6	3.3	0.09
2	321.2	6.5	2.0	0.9	0.76	2.2	17.5	13.0	4.8	0.10
3	53.6	5.9	2.5	0.7	0.63	3.4	8.0	6.4	3.5	0.14
4	58.8	5.2	1.0	1.0	0.51	2.8	3.2	4.6	4.5	0.10
1959										
1	53.9	5.5	1.3	0.7	0.46	2.7	5.0	3.6	4.7	0.10
2	505.0	6.8	1.1	0.8	0.69	3.1	24.8	25.9	9.2	0.08
3	61.6	5.7	1.6	0.8	0.64	4.0	14.7	4.5	5.1	0.09
4	75.8	6.0	1.4	0.8	0.52	4.5	3.8	6.8	2.4	0.07
1960										
1	366.4	5.9	1.1	0.4	0.68	3.4	15.5	17.8	4.4	0.09
2	105.0	5.2	2.5	1.0	0.62	4.7	7.5	7.7	4.3	0.12
3	69.4	6.0	0.9	1.1	0.61	3.7	6.0	7.5	3.8	0.09
4	33.5	7.0	1.9	0.8	0.55	2.8	3.5	2.3	3.5	0.12
1961										
1	46.6	6.3	1.1	0.7	0.59	3.2	3.2	3.6	5.5	0.09
2	291.0	6.4	1.6	0.8	0.59	6.2	10.2	17.0	5.5	0.08
3	294.0	5.7	1.1	0.9	0.52	2.6	13.8	26.3	3.8	0.06
4	87.9	7.7	2.0	0.8	1.46	1.9	12.3	8.0	7.5	0.09

Appendix C

NOTE ON AGENCY RATINGS AND "QUALITY" DISTRIBUTION

Each of the public offerings examined in Chapter 6 bore an agency rating at issue. The purpose of this note is to compare those agency ratings with the basic classes used in Chapters 3 and 4, above.

The procedure used, for the purpose of making this comparison, was as follows:

1. First, a seventh column was added to the two matrixes (Charts 6 and 13). This was done because many public offerings are issued by very large companies and the matrixes used to classify direct placements failed, to give full effect to this fact. The class interval over the next-to-last column became $135.1 million to $540.0 million instead of $135.1+, and the class interval over the last column became $540.0 million and over. In effect, therefore, those public offerings with total capitalization in excess of $540.0 million were ranked one class higher than would otherwise have been the case.

2. The public offerings in the sample were then deposited in the appropriate cells of the revised matrixes, and the class of each thus ascertained. This was done separately, of course, for industrials and utilities.

3. No attempt was made to average ratings when they differed as between the agencies: in all cases, the Standard and Poor's rating was used.[1]

4. The agency ratings and the classes were then cross-classified.

The results, which are given in Tables C-1, for industrials and C-2 for utilities, are of some interest. The percentages are calculated

[1] Translated into a Moody equivalent.

TABLE C-1

*Industrials: Distribution in Numbers
and Per Cent of Public Offerings by Agency
Rating and Direct Placement Class, 1951–61*

Agency Rating	Class					Total
	1	2	3	4	5–7	
AAA						
Number	14	--	--	--	--	14
Per cent	21.2	--	--	--	--	
AA						
Number	37	3	1	--	--	41
Per cent	56.1	7.9	1.7	--	--	
A						
Number	13	30	24	5	--	72
Per cent	19.7	78.9	41.4	19.2	--	
BAA						
Number	2	5	31	16	3	57
Per cent	3.0	13.2	53.4	61.5	30.0	
BA						
Number	--	--	2	5	7	14
Per cent	--	--	3.4	19.2	70.0	
Total						
Number	66	38	58	26	10	198
Per cent	100.0	100.0	100.0	100.0	100.0	

down the columns. Thus, of the sixty-six industrial public offerings which fell into class 1, fourteen (21.2 per cent) were rated Aaa by Standard and Poor's, thirty-seven (56.1 per cent) were rated AA, thirteen (19.7 per cent) were rated A, and two (3.0 per cent), Baa. The same procedure was followed for the other classes and for utilities.[2]

[2] The addition of one or two carefully selected variables would probably enable us to distinguish, with a much higher degree of accuracy, among the agency ratings.

TABLE C-2

Public Utilities: Distribution in Numbers and
Per Cent of Public Offerings by Agency Rating
and Direct Placement Class, 1951–61

Agency Rating	1	2	3	4	5	6–8	Total
AAA							
Number	37	2					
Per cent	44.6	3.2				――	30
AA							
Number	38	30	8	3	1		
Per cent	45.8	47.6	17.4	16.7	16.7	――	80
A							
Number	8	30	33	12	3	1	
Per cent	9.6	47.6	71.7	66.7	50.0	33.3	87
BAA							
Number		1	5	3	2		
Per cent	――	1.6	10.8	16.7	33.3	――	11
BA							
Number						2	
Per cent	――	――	――	――	――	66.7	2
Total							
Number	83	63	46	18	6	3	
Per cent	100.0	100.0	100.0	100.0	100.0	100.0	219

Table C-3 compares the "quality" distribution of public offerings with the "quality" distribution of direct placements—separately for industrials and utilities. The results should be interpreted with caution. The sample of direct placements is, presumably, representative, but public offerings of under $2 million of face amount were not included in the sample of public offerings. Subject to this caveat, three tentative conclusions emerge:

1. The average "quality" of public offerings is probably substantially higher than the average "quality" of direct placements—virtually all public offerings fall in classes 1 to 5, whereas 50.5

TABLE C-3

Comparative Distribution in Numbers and Per Cent of Public Offerings and Direct Placements, by Class, 1951–61

	Class						
	1	2	3	4	5	6–8	Total
Industrials							
Number							
Public offerings	66	38	58	26	10	––	198
Direct placements	61	110	233	311	329	400	1444
Per Cent							
Public offerings	33.3	19.2	29.3	13.1	5.1	––	100.0
Direct placements	4.2	7.6	16.1	21.5	22.8	27.7	100.0
Public Utilities							
Number							
Public offerings	83	63	46	18	6	3	219
Direct Placements	6	22	62	137	162	342	731
Per cent							
Public offerings	37.9	28.8	21.0	8.2	2.7	1.4	100.0
Direct Placements	0.8	3.0	8.5	18.7	22.2	46.8	100.0

per cent of industrial and 69.0 per cent of utility direct placements fall in class 5 and above.

2. The number of industrial direct placements vastly exceeds the number of industrial public offerings: the sample of the latter used constitutes virtually the whole universe of industrial public offerings sold, 1951–61, except, of course, for those of less than $2 million of face amount.[3]

3. The number of utility direct placements is not appreciably greater and may be smaller than the number of utility public offerings. (The sample of utility public offerings represented about 30 per cent of all those sold, 1951–61.)

[3] Convertible issues were not included.

Appendix D

REGRESSION COEFFICIENTS OF
SIGNIFICANT VARIABLES,
BY CROSS SECTION

TABLE D-1

Industrials: Estimates of Regression Parameters, Quarterly, 1951–61

Year and Quarter	b_1	σ_{b_1}	b_2	σ_{b_2}	b_3	σ_{b_3}	$b_{4(r)}$[a]	$\sigma_{b_{4(r)}}$[a]
1951								
1	-.0027	.0156	-.0789	.0827	-.0139	.0847	.0938	.0637
2	.0278	.0132	-.0499	.0451	.0865	.0038	.0029	.0405
3	-.0134	.0143	-.0656	.0271	-.0378	.0702	.1470	.0472
4	.0133	.0169	-.2466	.0501	.0062	.1311	.1896	.0505
1952								
1	.0238	.0151	-.1822	.0682	-.0813	.0809	.2034	.0555
2	-.0043	.0130	-.1153	.0902	-.0623	.0839	.1703	.0836
3	-.0027	.0133	-.3203	.1125	-.0660	.0832	.3319	.1164
4	.0461	.0323	-.1415	.0505	.1719	.1080	.0770	.0349
1953								
1	.0029	.0274	-.0681	.0789	-.0486	.1122	-.0047	.0641
2	.0232	.0123	-.1750	.0685	-.0456	.0532	.2017	.0752
3	.0203	.0199	+.0509	.1149	-.3628	.1713	-.0310	.1185
4	-.0094	.0133	+.0531	.0468	-.0505	.0674	.0815	.0398
1954								
1	-.0147	.0246	+.0043	.1036	-.3251	.1410	-.0273	.0892
2	.0114	.0139	-.0677	.0677	-.0195	.0764	.1043	.0556
3	.0038	.0235	-.0679	.0928	-.0448	.1097	.1329	.0904
4	-.0020	.0147	-.0061	.0579	.1477	.0963	.0337	.0549
1955								
1	.0240	.0282	-.1816	.0997	-.3038	.1175	.1267	.0786
2	-.0004	.0157	-.0280	.0691	.1263	.0963	.0374	.0476
3	-.0048	.0129	-.0594	.0441	.0206	.0871	.0089	.0192
4	.0024	.0180	-.0951	.0596	-.0871	.0792	.1095	.0584
1956								
1	.0148	.0189	+.0138	.0728	-.1670	.0846	-.0268	.0945
2	-.0027	.0185	+.0805	.0643	-.2740	.1106	-.0570	.0703
3	.0073	.0196	+.0168	.0352	.0091	.0800	.0444	.0360
4	-.0081	.0151	-.0751	.0576	-.0801	.0894	.0793	.0443
1957								
1	.0117	.0158	-.1218	.0593	-.1492	.1310	.1852	.0688
2	.0190	.0170	-.0550	.0407	.0213	.0739	.1033	.0390
3	-.0097	.1695	-.1453	.3205	-.3100	.1387	.1448	.9389
4	-.0211	.0364	-.0148	.1694	-.3670	.3161	-.0118	.0596

(continued)

TABLE D-1 (continued)

Year and Quarter	b_1	σ_{b_1}	b_2	σ_{b_2}	b_3	σ_{b_3}	$b_{4(r)}$[a]	$\sigma_{b_{4(r)}}$[a]
1958								
1	−.0418	.0178	+.0080	.0819	−.1352	.0907	.0367	.0790
2	−.0146	.0201	−.0795	.0558	−.0032	.0912	.1475	.0485
3	.0294	.0127	−.1457	.0703	−.0128	.0759	.1024	.0630
4	.0100	.0118	−.0018	.0249	−.3000	.1175	.0126	.0156
1959								
1	−.0415	.0690	−.1091	.2486	.3443	.4250	.2999	.4404
2	.0248	.0174	+.0053	.0701	−.0119	.0693	−.0321	.0568
3	−.0300	.0075	+.1129	.0478	.0585	.0387	−.0214	.0441
4	.0144	.0100	−.0626	.0716	−.0314	.0961	.0839	.0776
1960								
1	.0261	.0303	−.3085	.1698	.1143	.2581	.4060	.2274
2	.0031	.0346	+.0470	.1115	.2341	.2638	.0530	.1033
3	−.0284	.0258	+.0002	.0691	.2360	.1010	−.0357	.0558
4	−.0022	.0142	−.0790	.0437	−.1020	.0958	.0404	.0374
1961								
1	.0071	.0093	−.0884	.0833	−.0008	.0602	.1099	.0861
2	.0033	.0115	−.0040	.0512	−.0350	.1044	.0719	.0392
3	−.0149	.0228	−.0538	.0574	.1221	.0711	.0549	.0411
4	.0449	.0655	+.0613	.0792	−.0093	.1953	−.0463	.0949

Year and Quarter	b_5	σ_{b_5}	b_6	σ_{b_6}	b_7	σ_{b_7}	b_8	σ_{b_8}
1951								
1	−.0305	.0167	−.0430	.0306	−.0006	.0020	−.0387	.0215
2	−.0689	.0207	−.0283	.0256	.0025	.0020	−.0161	.0283
3	−.0342	.0164	.0295	.0248	−.0025	.0015	−.0275	.0194
4	.0184	.0200	−.0526	.0243	−.0033	.0014	+.0213	.0266
1952								
1	−.0360	.0170	−.0048	.0240	.0008	.0013	−.0478	.0168
2	−.0428	.0198	−.0014	.0254	.0031	.0016	+.0036	.0159
3	−.0255	.0144	−.0112	.0266	−.0001	.0021	−.0326	.0155
4	−.0454	.0228	−.0535	.0394	.0025	.0030	+.0386	.0279

(continued)

TABLE D-1 (continued)

Year and Quarter	b_5	σ_{b_5}	b_6	σ_{b_6}	b_7	σ_{b_7}	b_8	σ_{b_8}
1953								
1	-.0557	.0254	-.0654	.0345	.0052	.0032	+.0312	.0299
2	-.0371	.0134	.0053	.0214	-.0021	.0023	-.0580	.0223
3	-.0414	.0318	.0277	.0308	.0019	.0022	+.0055	.0452
4	.0252	.0110	.0408	.0255	.0009	.0017	-.0100	.0166
1954								
1	-.0319	.0248	-.0609	.0436	.0025	.0022	+.0270	.0389
2	-.0365	.0154	-.0251	.0275	.0046	.0022	-.0695	.0166
3	-.0323	.0167	-.0580	.0280	-.0004	.0015	-.0337	.0159
4	-.0538	.0186	-.0587	.0271	.0036	.0018	-.0159	.0119
1955								
1	.0103	.0232	-.0381	.0397	.0015	.0030	-.0255	.0359
2	-.0014	.0152	-.0210	.0308	.0011	.0019	-.0589	.0271
3	-.0542	.0219	-.0234	.0270	-.0003	.0030	+.0004	.0260
4	-.0547	.0182	.0080	.0310	-.0002	.0022	-.0002	.0211
1956								
1	-.0254	.0352	.0114	.0432	-.0006	.0028	-.0006	.0335
2	.0095	.0197	.0230	.0250	.0035	.0023	-.0950	.0249
3	-.0150	.0186	-.0475	.0246	-.0060	.0019	-.0180	.0151
4	.0114	.0142	.0203	.0266	.0021	.0021	-.0545	.0232
1957								
1	-.0296	.0166	-.0080	.0256	.0005	.0018	-.0166	.0137
2	-.0130	.0158	-.0526	.0248	.0002	.0023	-.0047	.0161
3	b	b	-.0456	.0346	-.0080	.0122	+.0734	.2379
4	-.0204	.1254	-.0545	.0926	.0054	.0096	+.0041	.1290
1958								
1	-.0206	.0214	-.0392	.0253	.0042	.0029	-.0261	.0167
2	-.0152	.0163	-.0044	.0321	.0027	.0022	-.0205	.0112
3	-.0226	.0151	.0466	.0221	.0009	.0016	+.0520	.0142
4	.0031	.0208	-.0204	.0268	-.0002	.0016	-.0080	.0165
1959								
1	.0074	.1019	-.0547	.1064	.0002	.0060	+.0144	.0585
2	-.0110	.0139	.0044	.0274	.0004	.0029	-.0078	.0148
3	-.0050	.0088	-.0274	.0140	.0005	.0008	-.0246	.0103
4	-.0091	.0251	.0466	.0321	.0062	.0028	-.0556	.0243

(continued)

TABLE D-1 (continued)

Year and Quarter	b_5	σ_{b_5}	b_6	σ_{b_6}	b_7	σ_{b_7}	b_8	σ_{b_8}
1960								
1	-.0286	.0511	-.0065	.0783	-.0046	.0078	-.0127	.0290
2	-.0031	.0427	-.0568	.0584	.0020	.0045	-.0543	.0425
3	-.0164	.0314	.0449	.0457	.0013	.0029	+.0225	.0168
4	-.0300	.0238	-.0102	.0265	.0027	.0024	+.0224	.0155
1961								
1	-.0088	.0118	.0111	.0190	-.0018	.0016	-.0166	.0115
2	-.0024	.0161	-.0122	.0229	-.0001	.0021	+.0024	.0150
3	.0088	.0309	.0210	.0282	-.0019	.0022	-.0298	.0302
4	-.0419	.0431	.0332	.0808	-.0039	.0070	-.0660	.0399

Year and Quarter	b_{12}	$\sigma_{b_{12}}$	b_{13}	$\sigma_{b_{13}}$	b_{15}	$\sigma_{b_{15}}$
1951						
1	-.0209	.0446	-.0998	.1017	-.0462	.0780
2	-.0282	.0320	-.1277	.0913	.0244	.0463
3	-.0982	.0402	.0604	.0841	-.1287	.0549
4	-.0289	.0279	.1327	.1660	-.0714	.0771
1952						
1	-.0309	.0298	.1096	.1163	-.0486	.0615
2	-.0827	.0333	-.0061	.0947	-.1038	.0847
3	-.0085	.0217	.0718	.0777	-.2875	.0955
4	.0029	.0296	-.3048	.1544	.0496	.0607
1953						
1	-.0005	.0305	-.0625	.1384	-.0408	.0787
2	.0044	.0176	.0159	.0631	-.0892	.0640
3	-.0410	.0424	.1044	.1894	.0720	.1118
4	-.0379	.0250	-.0663	.0882	-.0211	.0333
1954						
1	-.0327	.0534	.2403	.1890	.0632	.0709
2	-.0243	.0278	-.0547	.0922	.0006	.0626
3	-.0773	.0288	.1161	.1240	-.1196	.0862
4	-.0624	.0230	-.2777	.1109	.0295	.0614

(continued)

Appendix D

TABLE D-1 (concluded)

Year and Quarter	b_{12}	$\sigma_{b_{12}}$	b_{13}	$\sigma_{b_{13}}$	b_{15}	$\sigma_{b_{15}}$
1955						
1	.0211	.0516	.1966	.1125	-.0359	.0808
2	-.0188	.0291	-.1198	.1100	.1093	.0739
3	-.0297	.0284	.0338	.0966	.0126	.0407
4	-.0352	.0232	-.0167	.0789	-.0985	.0551
1956						
1	-.0218	.0368	.2577	.0897	.0493	.0738
2	.0303	.0258	.2551	.1433	.1422	.0719
3	-.0695	.0268	.0307	.1258	-.0193	.0346
4	.0157	.0373	-.0271	.1239	.0173	.0452
1957						
1	-.0560	.0365	.1386	.1372	-.1390	.0754
2	-.0564	.0288	.0228	.0874	-.0911	.0426
3	-.1747	.2968	.5209	.5260	-.2099	.7195
4	-.0371	.0619	.4463	.2901	.0498	.1408
1958						
1	-.0564	.0379	.0748	.1452	.0073	.0710
2	-.0723	.0241	-.0924	.0850	-.1574	.0471
3	-.0054	.0335	-.0485	.1094	-.1389	.0704
4	-.0301	.0190	.2637	.1409	.0492	.0277
1959						
1	-.1873	.2078	-.3325	.4843	-.3158	.4500
2	.0113	.0359	-.0023	.0867	-.0016	.0482
3	-.1013	.0170	.0156	.0479	.0463	.0445
4	-.0024	.0249	-.0744	.0991	.0152	.0770
1960						
1	-.0648	.1115	-.1440	.2402	-.4459	.2886
2	-.0981	.0644	-.2265	.3109	.0539	.1062
3	-.0188	.0347	-.2315	.1429	.0380	.0645
4	.0161	.0253	-.0778	.0877	-.0386	.0441
1961						
1	-.0276	.0200	-.0785	.0491	-.0250	.0842
2	-.0736	.0294	-.0270	.0859	-.0301	.0531
3	-.0146	.0416	-.0841	.0723	-.0323	.0653
4	.0144	.0662	-.1513	.2091	.1174	.1207

[a]Redefined variable; for explanation see Chapter 3.
[b]Singular matrix.

TABLE D-2

Public Utilities: Estimates of Regression Parameters, Semiannually, 1951−61

	b_1	σ_{b_1}	b_2	σ_{b_2}	b_3	σ_{b_3}	$b_{4(r)}$[a]	$\sigma_{b_{4(r)}}$[a]
1951								
1	.0378	.0343	−.2826	.1842	−.3763	.1364	−.0069	.1518
2	−.0077	.0173	−.1899	.1176	−.2475	.0816	.1518	.1133
1952								
1	−.0005	.0227	−.4198	.2163	−.2532	.2099	.3765	.1972
2	.0337	.0174	−.3104	.0962	−.1839	.0618	.2787	.1096
1953								
1	.0106	.0240	−.1161	.0754	−.0760	.0899	.1189	.0971
2	−.0286	.0144	−.0746	.0733	−.1126	.0667	.0239	.0612
1954								
1	−.0154	.0189	−.3397	.1375	−.0426	.1185	.2639	.1124
2	−.0055	.0141	−.3517	.1362	−.2230	.0867	.3067	.1376
1955								
1	−.0010	.0149	−.1129	.0775	−.2292	.0704	.1624	.0783
2	−.0058	.0146	−.1730	.0967	−.1079	.0577	.1440	.0792
1956								
1	.0180	.0322	−.1770	.1321	−.0147	.1524	.2584	.1361
2	−.0038	.0122	−.0862	.0687	−.0749	.0504	.1629	.0639
1957								
1	−.0102	.0088	−.0248	.0295	−.1730	.0400	.0248	.0230
2	−.0055	.0087	−.0591	.0480	−.0300	.0451	.0828	.0471
1958								
1	.0043	.0183	+.1291	.0916	−.1908	.0917	−.0760	.0895
2	.0206	.0177	−.2857	.1091	−.0351	.0766	.3025	.1100
1959								
1	−.0092	.0116	+.0613	.0584	−.0528	.0603	.0080	.0547
2	.0091	.0186	+.0176	.0848	−.0757	.1181	−.0856	.1034
1960								
1	.0104	.0061	−.0774	.0398	−.0457	.0352	.0905	.0364
2	−.0062	.0145	−.0439	.0654	−.1001	.0468	−.0083	.0548
1961								
1	−.0031	.0074	+.0233	.0456	−.0466	.0459	−.0023	.0384
2	.0066	.0140	−.1832	.1386	−.3368	.1036	.2895	.1600

(continued)

TABLE D-2 (continued)

		b_5	σ_{b_5}	b_6	σ_{b_6}	b_7	σ_{b_7}	b_8	σ_{b_8}
1951									
	1	−.0086	.0435	−.0862	.0466	−.0105	.0120	+.0414	.0532
	2	.0440	.0263	−.0446	.0369	.0019	.0024	−.0295	.0243
1952									
	1	−.0018	.0411	−.0412	.0613	−.0274	.0363	+.0134	.0385
	2	.0192	.0109	.0011	.0304	.0070	.0009	.0204	.0170
1953									
	1	.0149	.0242	.0100	.0254	.0174	.0065	+.0016	.0252
	2	.0297	.0252	−.0017	.0243	.0079	.0051	+.0049	.0254
1954									
	1	.0196	.0310	−.0085	.0347	−.0025	.0023	+.0745	.0248
	2	.0738	.0346	.0765	.0328	−.0025	.0024	+.0020	.0165
1955									
	1	.0042	.0144	−.0049	.0235	.0032	.0132	−.0069	.0188
	2	−.0111	.0181	−.0304	.0280	.0019	.0031	+.0027	.0195
1956									
	1	.0186	.0353	−.0596	.0642	.0035	.0086	+.0340	.0370
	2	.0035	.0142	.0033	.0203	.0047	.0025	+.0066	.0152
1957									
	1	.0151	.0084	−.0454	.0185	.0030	.0021	−.0094	.0109
	2	−.0116	.0085	−.0203	.0186	.0046	.0024	−.0479	.0151
1958									
	1	.0273	.0219	.0092	.0318	.0036	.0057	−.0425	.0206
	2	−.0028	.0187	−.0399	.0248	.0013	.0041	−.0086	.0225
1959									
	1	.0079	.0149	.0330	.0222	−.0013	.0031	−.0421	.0182
	2	.0049	.0233	−.0252	.0409	.0008	.0033	−.0074	.0220
1960									
	1	.0360	.0078	−.0289	.0142	−.0017	.0013	−.0220	.0082
	2	−.0003	.0091	−.0484	.0197	.0012	.0026	−.0026	.0179
1961									
	1	.0132	.0084	.0049	.0131	.0009	.0013	−.0374	.0108
	2	.0068	.0156	−.0102	.0215	−.0177	.0073	−.0549	.0219

(continued)

TABLE D-2 (concluded)

	b_{12}	$\sigma_{b_{12}}$	b_{13}	$\sigma_{b_{13}}$	b_{15}	$\sigma_{b_{15}}$
1951						
1	.1164	.0780	.3354	.1398	-.0763	.1188
2	.0067	.0421	.1284	.1052	-.0600	.1254
1952						
1	.0020	.0611	.2576	.3105	-.2550	.2957
2	-.0277	.0490	.1378	.0888	-.2286	.1240
1953						
1	-.0205	.0389	-.0357	.1087	-.0332	.1125
2	-.0486	.0295	.1254	.1052	-.0003	.0967
1954						
1	-.0437	.0470	.1214	.1707	-.2469	.1465
2	-.0067	.0330	.3787	.0950	-.3391	.1604
1955						
1	-.0517	.0265	.0420	.1120	-.1395	.0896
2	.0122	.0317	.0144	.0763	-.0613	.0810
1956						
1	-.0494	.0482	-.2204	.3051	-.1490	.1848
2	.0018	.0294	-.0046	.0591	-.1498	.0672
1957						
1	.0172	.0162	-.0143	.0489	.0283	.0404
2	.0010	.0248	-.0847	.0591	.0901	.0667
1958						
1	-.1103	.0392	.1686	.1728	.0544	.1410
2	-.0221	.0312	-.2173	.1539	-.2321	.1102
1959						
1	-.0661	.0315	.0967	.0670	.0537	.0609
2	-.0166	.0403	.0161	.1243	.1606	.1121
1960						
1	.0060	.0164	-.0517	.0427	.1360	.0398
2	-.0523	.0247	-.2527	.0902	.0154	.0694
1961						
1	-.0141	.0216	.0292	.0735	.1832	.0452
2	-.0823	.0325	.3943	.1585	-.2268	.1922

[a]Redefined variable; for explanation see Chapter 3.

*Industrials: Partial Regression of Yield on Significant
Variables, Quarterly, 1951–61*

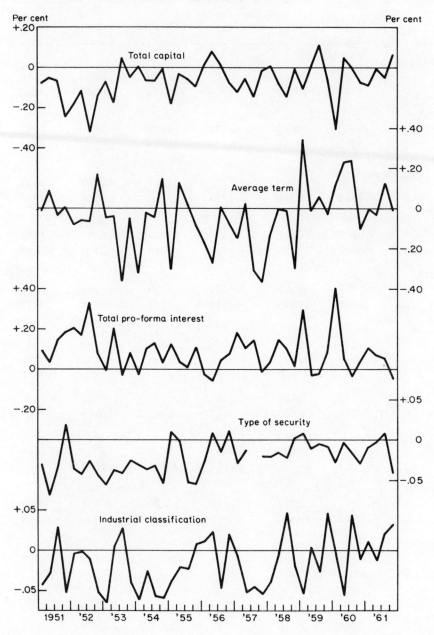

CHART D-1 (concluded)

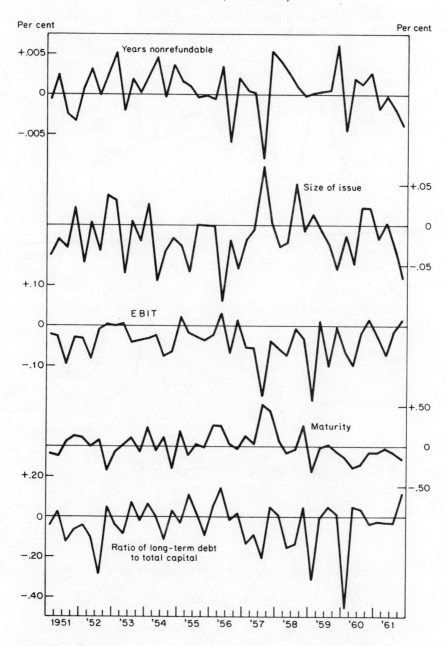

Public Utilities: Partial Regression of Yield on Significant Variables, Semiannually, 1951–61

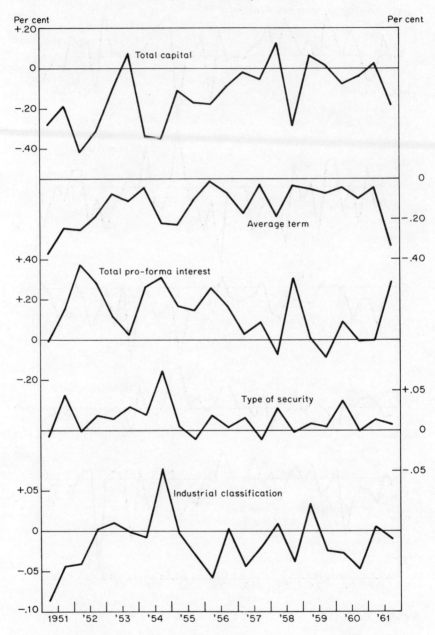

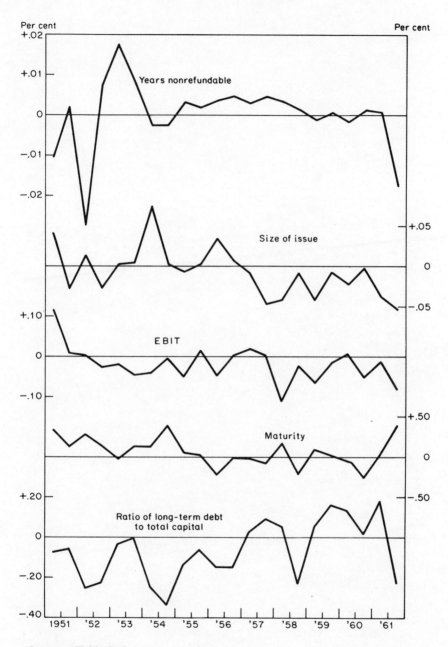

SOURCE: Table D-2.

INDEX

Average size of issue, definition of, as variable, 18
See also Variables used to determine yield
Average term:
as yield-determining variable, 18
definition of, as variable, 29
See also Variables used to determine yield

Capitalization, total pro-forma:
as measure of size of company, 18
definition of, as variable, 34
role of, in cross-classified series, 39
See also Variables used to determine yield
Cohan, A. B., 4n, 5n, 7n
Company size, see Size of company
Corey, R. E., 4n, 10n
Cross-section multiple regression as procedure used, 27–28
Coverage, as combined variable, 41
See also Variables used to determine yield

Depreciation charges, 37n
Direct placements:
bank term loans and, 9, 10
classes of, 25
data available on, 7
definition of, 1, 8–9, 11
growth of:
absolute, 1
consequences of, 4–7
industrial, see Industrial direct placements, growth of
in relation to public offerings, 1, 8–9, 125–134
in relation to total cash debt offerings, 1
utility, see Public utility direct placements, growth of
mortgages and, 9, 10
of benevolent associations, 10, 11, 13

Direct placements (cont.)
of life insurance companies, 10, 11, 13
of mutual funds, 10, 13
of pension funds, 10, 11, 13
pure debt corporate, 11
quality of, 25
rail, see rail direct placements
See also Finance company direct placements; Industrial direct placements; Public utility direct placements

Earnings before interest and taxes (EBIT):
as yield-determining variable, 18
definition of, as variable, 30
dispersion of, as variable, 31
ratio of, to interest, 30–31
See also Times charges earned; Variables used to determine yield
Earnings, growth in, see Growth in earnings
Earnings, variability in, see Variability in earnings
Electric companies, see Public utilities, yield series

FHA mortgages:
compared with industrial series, 41–42, 71–72
compared with utilities series, 84, 106
Finance company direct placements:
amount of, in sample, 16, 17
characteristics of, compared with others, 114
IDD yield and size-of-issue series, 15
industrial classification of, 34
significant variables, 115
behavior of, 149
correlations of, 116–121
yield series:
average quarterly, 19, 115, 122–124